1·59

ASTON V
GREA

ASTON VILLA GREATS

Leon Hickman

SPORTSPRINT PUBLISHING
EDINBURGH

ISBN 0 85976 313 7

Phototypeset by Beecee Typesetting Services
Printed in Great Britain by Bell & Bain Ltd., Glasgow

Contents

Acknowledgements

I wish to thank Aston Villa FC, players and staff, who have been so helpful to me in producing this book. My thanks also go to Eric Houghton, Ron Wylie and the former players who were receptive to my task. Special thanks to Rob Bishop who read the manuscript and made a number of constructive suggestions and to Tony Matthews for some of the statistics.

L.H.

CHAPTER 1

Introduction

FOR MANY YEARS ASTON VILLA FOUND IT AS difficult to live with tradition as generations of their players did to create it. The laurels won by men in baggy shorts before the First World War, and to a lesser extent in the years up to the Second, have not rested comfortably on the brows of their successors. In the past 45 years fine footballers and illustrious deeds have shared the Villa Park stage with men of modest talent involved in grim misfortune.

Yet the torch of this great club, lit 116 years ago under a gas lamp in Heathfield Road, Lozells, then on the outskirts of the city of a thousand trades, has always burned proudly for football and for Birmingham. Which other club, foisted with Third Division football by process of complacency and weariness, could have summoned 48,110 spectators for a mid-February match with Bournemouth, as Villa did in 1972? The power of the people was made manifest, a damburst of passion that was to sweep Villa beyond the League championship and to the European Cup in ten sweet years.

Asked to select the ten outstanding players of the post-war era, I suppose the easiest option would have been to name Jimmy Rimmer (or Nigel Spink), Kenny Swain, Gary Williams, Allan Evans, Ken McNaught, Dennis Mortimer, Des Bremner, Gary Shaw, Peter Withe, Gordon Cowans and Tony Morley and then to puzzle for a couple of weeks about which two to leave out. No Villa fan needs reminding that this was the team who on 26 May 1982, won the European Cup, nor, I think, that this was the best side that ever wore the claret and blue.

Three of these men are included: skipper Mortimer, the Rotterdam scorer Withe and, not surprisingly, Gordon Cowans. It was with sadness, however, that I felt I had to reject the claims of Evans, particularly, for he was one of about half-a-dozen exclusions with whom the faithful Villa fan may legitimately argue. Evans played nearly 500 games for Villa, represented Scotland in the World Cup in Spain, and remained as honest a player as you would find in a long search through League annals.

Villa have always been serviced admirably by Scots, even before Jimmy Cowan, known as 'the Prince of Half-backs', represented his country against England in 1896, six years after moving to the Birmingham club from Vale of Leven Reserves. Cowan played 354 times for Villa with whom he won five League championship honours, from 1894-1900, two F.A. Cup winners medals, a losers' medal and, most peculiarly, the Powderhall Sprint Handicap of 1896. For this offence, he was fined and suspended by a furious club committee who, however, were sufficiently calculating to ensure he was available in the 1896-97 season when their team recorded the League and Cup double.

Newcomers to the Villa shrine will surely gasp at this record, rivalling any until Liverpool arrived to dominate the most recent 25 years of English football. Just as Bill Shankly, as manager, set the agenda for Liverpool's pre-eminence, so the empire builder at Villa was another Scot of immense force and magnetism, George Burrell Ramsey, player, secretary and vice-president over 59 years of service. An immaculate dresser who favoured a bow-tie and striped shirt, Ramsey had shunned the poor streets of the Cathcart area of Glasgow to become a tricky ball-player with Villa, his visibility greatly heightened by the polo cap on his head and long pants that brushed his calves. He was born to be a star and, fortunately for Villa, he chose to

European Cup hoisted around the streets of Birmingham.

be a satellite of the club, along with such fervently active pioneers as William McGregor, founder of the Football League, Archie Hunter, Frederick Rinder and John Lindsay, all of whom were instrumental in the purchase of Villa Park in 1896.

It is not difficult to imagine the pride these men would have had in the European Cup triumph, although by the time Ramsey died in 1935, he had seen Villa win the F.A. Cup and the Championship six times each. In the years between the founding of the League in 1888-89, and Ramsey's demise, Villa were out of the top ten of the league only seven times in 43 seasons. To old men who grew up in these noble times, the recent habit of disregarding Villa as outside 'the Big Five' is an impertinence of considerable magnitude.

Once their colic has subsided, they may be prepared to acknowledge — indeed, they may taunt younger supporters with the knowledge — that Villa have not consistently for half a century been what they were. The truth is that only ten men have been capped for England — four of these for one match or less — since 1946, while 42 appeared in national colours before Hitler strutted to war. My task in choosing the ten would have been much more perplexing, therefore, had it been necessary in, say, 1939.

Even so, the years since have been as alive as a Renoir scene with colour and vivid incident. The club have been champions of the First, Second and Third Divisions, they have won the F.A. Cup once, the Football League Cup (or whatever sponsors called it) three times, the European Cup once and the European Super Cup once. It is a record to be respected, yet it has been compiled in brief bursts of fruitful years after long periods of fallowness. Power battles have not helped, either, and whatever the general attitude to the current chairman, Doug Ellis, he has at least brought back stability and purposefulness to Villa Park.

In his three periods as chairman, Ellis has appointed seven managers, Tommy Docherty, Vic Crowe, Ron Saunders, Graham Turner, Billy McNeill, Graham Taylor and Jozef Venglos. Two of these, Saunders and Taylor, have been successful and one, Crowe, fairly so. In other words, the most important task a chairman has to perform is to appoint a manager. He must then stand back and allow him to manage.

By very different methods, Saunders and Taylor were able to manoeuvre room for themselves and in doing so transformed a club dangerously adrift into a winner or major contender. Players' skills were illuminated by the light these managers created and it is no accident that in the past season, under Taylor, as manager, five first-team men were recognised by England, David Platt in the senior team, Cowans and Tony Daley in the B team and Mark Blake and Ian Olney in the under-21s. In the European Cup-winning side, there were six: Spink, Withe, Cowans, Morley in the seniors, Mortimer in the

B and Shaw under-21. Altogether five of these eleven are among my Aston Villa Greats.

It needs no explanation from me as to why I chose Cowans, certainly the best passer of a ball I have seen in a Villa shirt. Brave and inexhaustible, too, he epitomises the finest in football. Platt describes him as 'the best footballer I have played with,' and England must have had an exceptional team in the World Cup for Cowans to have been left behind. Cowans must sometimes wonder whether it pays to be as self-effacing as he is. Perhaps a tantrum or two, the odd well-publicised incident in a nightclub or even a toss of his shirt into the dug-out would have drawn the extra bit of attention to him. Not for 'Sid', though: he reserves his showmanship for the football field.

David Platt is in the ten because he is far too good a player to be left out. The temptation to call him a jack of all trades should be resisted because of the implication that he is master of none, whereas he has proved to be a spectacular goalscorer for Villa and England, an athlete and competitor of the highest order. His test comes over the next few seasons during which he will be trying to emulate John Wark in continuing regularly to strike goals of lightning, rather than Glenn Hoddle, for whom the streak faded prematurely. Not that Platt is a copy of either: Wark's scoring was born of instinct, Hoddle's of virtuosity, Platt's of a scent for expanding space in the penalty area. This, surely, is a gift shared with Bryan Robson, the man in the No. 7 shirt upon which Platt himself places so much value.

Cast away by Manchester United at 19, Platt was fortunate that his apprenticeship at Crewe, late as it was, and his graduation at Villa have taken place under the guidance of Dario Gradi and Graham Taylor, managers who relish moulding young players into disciplined professionals. Platt's talent to be many things on a football field demands, it may seem paradoxically, pre-planning of a far more subtle kind than for, say, Steve Hodge whose role as a left-side support man is easily understood. Last season, Villa in their best spell were fashioned around Platt's flexibility. England may well be, shortly, one day, too.

Only one other central figure of this book played League football last season, and that in itself is something of a wonder unless you happen to know Peter Withe. Assistant manager at Huddersfield, Withe appeared as emergency sweeper, a 38-year-old veteran in whom the flames of competition still burn hot. Ten years ago last summer, Ron Saunders scooped a posse of managers to persuade the lean Liverpudlian to become the Clint Eastwood of Villa Park and clean up a few gongs. Good and Bad, Withe could always be. But Ugly? Well, only to opponents.

The story has it that Saunders was reluctant at first to bid for Withe who had reached the end of his contract at Newcastle. I can only believe this was true because Saunders knew that the centre-forward he signed in May, 1980, would be the pivotal figure in his improving team and naturally enough, had initial fears. Clearly, he swallowed them quickly for he moved with typical speed to snatch the player from Everton's grasp. In two decades as a manager, Saunders was never better rewarded. Withe's part in Villa's first championship in 71 years was colossal. That he scored the European Cup winner was absolutely just. That he nearly missed it, absolutely denied!

Which brings us tidily to Dennis Mortimer, skipper of the side in the two years that nearly put them among the Big Five, according to those pillars of football judgment, ITV. Mortimer was among Saunders's other inspired signings, another Liverpudlian whose record, astonishingly, shows no England appearances.

When Morty joined Villa in 1975, he was freely spoken of as a future international. In the next ten years he improved consistently until, in the great years of the early Eighties, he was peerless as a fetcher and carrier, acute in tactical awareness and with a precious yard of pace that made him lethal breaking from midfield.

Villa fans are still saddened by Mortimer's break with the

The Villa's European squad.

club, in many ways similar to that of Charlie Aitken, another of my choices. But when in the not-too-distant future boys are asked to name the European Cup team, it will be Mortimer's name first, I fancy, because he epitomised the professionalism that carried his team through the shock departure of manager Ron Saunders and on to the Feyenoord Stadium, Rotterdam. Probably the oddest outcome of Mortimer's disaffection with Villa is that he now works as a community officer with West Bromwich Albion, four miles away.

Brian Little and Andy Gray struck a glancing partnership that scattered sparks through the First Division and faded almost as quickly as it had appeared. The season of 1976-77 leaves a scorch mark, nevertheless, for in Little and Gray, Villa at last found two goalscorers rich in style and glamour. Even the London press could not keep its eyes from the perfection of Little's running and the dash of his fair-haired Scottish friend. They devastated good teams, Arsenal went down 5-1 at Villa Park, and so, far more extraordinarily, did Liverpool. Gray 2, Deehan 2 and Little were the scorers in a first half that tested belief. The Liverpool team contained nine England internationals and went on to win the League and European Cup and were finalists in the F.A. Cup. Villa (one England international, Little, and that for only 18 minutes) nervously secured the Football League Cup and, perhaps the most amazing fact of all, only Mortimer and Colin Gibson played in the side who won the championship four years later.

By then, Little had been forced by incurable knee problems to leave the game, while Gray was helping Wolves to an F.A. Cup semi-final place, having scored the only goal of the League Cup victory a year earlier. It was an ignominious ending to a fleeting but brilliant encounter by two magical figures in the Villa landscape. My feelings are as ambivalent as everyone else's about Saunders's treatment of them, yet the Czar of Villa Park had only to point to results to answer his detractors. But results aren't everything, are they?

Charlie Aitken bridged the worst years in the club's history, from Division One with Joe Mercer to Division One with Saunders by way of Dick Taylor, Tommy Cummings, Tommy Docherty, and Vic Crowe, into the Second and Third Divisions and back again. Turbulent, tumultuous years, these. Aitken, a man of Edinburgh brought up to play rugby, has a unique place in Villa history, having passed the great Billy Walker's record for most appearances, 659 of them in all. Aitken was an observer of the dramas that unfolded in his 16 years in Birmingham, an apparently permanent fixture among the disintegration and reconstruction, as quiet men in collars and ties became angry citizens of Aston Villa, helplessly watching as one of the most famous clubs in the land slipped from apathy to panic.

Yet in those years, Villa fans discovered two important qualities, one abstract, the other very tangible. Humility and democracy are not always bedfellows, but out of the realisation that it was the club's divine right to belong to the elite came the understanding that they could do something about it. The public responded in their thousands to a shares issue and, thus armed with a financial as well as a personal interest, initially were a force to be reckoned with. People's power failed to last the Seventies and, indeed, today the club's controlling interest is held by Doug Ellis who has said he no longer believes in democracy in football. Aitken, I suspect, would agree with him, although both would accept that there is an even greater democracy at work should Villa collapse again — the right of supporters to vote with their pockets and stay away.

Here I feel I must make an admission, for while the task of selecting ten men must be personal, idiosyncratic and, to some extent, invidious, nothing gave me graver concern than to omit Peter McParland. Now I know how Sir Alf Ramsey felt when he left Jimmy Greaves out of the 1966 World Cup final line-up.

There were many other players whose claims were checked and reviewed, besides those of the European Cup team.

In recent times, Tony Daley, Mark Walters, Alan McInally and Paul McGrath; two steps further back to Bruce Rioch, Ray Graydon, Chris Nicholl, John Gidman; then to the generation of Mick Wright, Tony Hateley, Ron Wylie, Harry Burrows, Alan Deakin, John Sleeuwenhoek, Derek Dougan and Phil Woosnam; in the F.A. Cup-winning era Vic Crowe, Peter Aldis, Jimmy Dugdale, Nigel Sims; finally, to the post-war period of Con Martin, Tommy Thompson, Harry Parkes, Danny Blanchflower, Frank Moss, Trevor Ford, George Edwards and George Cummings. Forgive me if I have missed one of your favourites, but of these McParland had a contribution to rival those of the three who actually completed the chapters, Stan Lynn, Gerry Hitchens and Johnny Dixon.

McParland will be best remembered for the winning goals he scored in the 1957 F.A. Cup final, having earlier collided with Ray Wood in the sixth minute. Wood was absent from the Manchester United goal when McParland effectively won Villa's first trophy in 37 years and the Old Trafford thousands were joined by most of the country in their condemnation of the Irish winger. If this incident implies that McParland was powerful, aggressive and unquenchable, then the impression is accurate. If it suggests ruthlessness or cynicism, then that is far from the truth. McParland's act in charging Wood had to be seen in the context of the times, for in those days goalkeepers were fair game. My own view was that he allowed enthusiasm to stray into recklessness but, then, whenever McParland appeared in the penalty area there was the sniff of fear in defenders' nostrils.

In all, McParland played 340 times for Villa, scoring 120 goals. He was capped 34 times for Northern Ireland. No-one would deny his right to be in a Villa Hall of Fame.

Lynn was a full back with claims to having the hardest shot in football, once scored a hat-trick and still laughs when reminded that George Cummings reckoned he was England material if only he had kicked the ball properly. In Lynn's day, full backs were not supposed to show much guile, most of them glorying in the fact that at one time or another they had knocked Matthews or Finney into touch — or so they said. Lynn was as hard as any but, booked only once in his life, had as sound a sense of fair play as you would expect in a well brought-up Lancashire lad.

His goals were legendary. One weighty swing at a solid caseball and a penalty kick would threaten to decapitate the opposition goalkeeper. Lynn was 33 when he left Villa, and still had time to play 148 times for Birmingham City, tormenting goalkeepers with 30 more goals.

Gerry Hitchens spent only four seasons with the club, yet for all his travels in Italy, where he is remembered as the epitome of English centre-forwards, he will always be chiefly associated with Villa. It was here that he scored 42 goals in his final season, his pace, persistence, strength and brave heart raising him to hero status at the Holte End. An unassuming miner's son, Hitchens' nearest Villa equivalent was Andy Gray. Fair-haired like Gray, he was more ruthless in his use of the ball, less spectacularly eager to pursue any cause, yet both became cult figures on the triumphs of one season.

By contrast, Dixon spent 15 years in the first team and,

incidentally, was just as angry as Aitken and Mortimer to have been elbowed out. A Geordie with a touch of the ball as deft as his fellow Tynesider Little's, Dixon was typical of the inside-forwards of his day. To suggest that men who linked the half-back positions with the act of scoring were commonplace for their skill and industry — often requiring the protection of more boisterous colleagues — is in no way to debase the position. The very opposite, for inside-forwards were the artists of football and if your club hadn't one, then the chances of it remaining in the First Division were nil. For 13 of those years, then, Dixon played the role of creator, his brush-strokes as gently applied as a water colourist's, and managed to strike a fair share of goals, too. 28 in 43 matches was his highest total in a season, 1951-52, when Villa finished sixth in Division One, the best they were to do in 43 years.

Dixon spanned the period from the start of the season after the war, skippered the 1957 F.A. Cup-winning side, and lasted into the Macmillan era of 'never had it so good.' Not true of Villa, however, for although his last and only match of the 1960-61 season established them in 9th position in the First Division, they had been relegated the season before for only the second time in their history and were about to embark on an unhappy decade which ended in tears and, humiliatingly, Division Three.

Each of the ten played a significant part in Villa's destiny, some rewarded with trophies, caps and medals, others with the adulation of supporters. The one unifying factor, I think, is that each never failed to give of his best.

I have structured this book to cover the entire 45 years since League football re-started, years of wide fluctuations at Villa Park. There have ben 13 managers in that time and probably as many chairmen. When Alex Massie quietly assumed the manager's position in September 1945 it signified no more than that he would be the first among equals, a kind of non-playing captain who, often uneasily, also acted as agent to the boardroom with responsibility for keeping the players content and the team in the First Division. There was no such thing as player-power, either in wage bargaining or in policy. In another way, though, the players had far more responsibility. When they played badly, it wasn't always the manager's fault, because he was purely regarded as the man who picked the team, not as the guide, guru and genius to be artificially applauded or sacrifically sacked, according to temporary success rating.

Yes, of course, managers were dismissed, as Massie was in 1950, but this was not accompanied by wailing or a gnashing of teeth. The players just got on with the season on the principle that this was another fine mess they had got themselves into. Interestingly, this relationship with the management staff was briefly revived when Tony Barton took over from Saunders — and Villa won the European Cup.

It is fair to say that in those years after the war, the board were prepared to settle for lower standards than they should have. Villa became fossilised, a relic of what it was when men of Ramsey's stamp made it the greatest club name in the world. For years it wasn't even the best in the West Midlands: Wolves and West Bromwich brimmed with success in the Black Country, Birmingham City had a fine side in the second half of the Fifties and followed Wolves' example by installing floodlights. The Villa board's lack of illuminating thought was never better exemplified than in their reluctance to fit lights.

Kindly Eric Houghton and his tough trainer Bill Moore put together a side who won the F.A. Cup but Houghton lasted only 18 further months before Joe Mercer took over and was brought to the brink of a nervous breakdown by his six years in the job. Villa were stuck with the 'off with his head' syndrome that runs thus: board appoints manager . . . manager fails to correct in a year the slide that has been going on for 20 . . . board claim they have done everything possible to support manager . . . fans cry for manager's head . . . and, duly, it is delivered on a platter.

Dick Taylor, Tommy Cummings and Tommy Docherty,

Cheers to the League title! Highbury, 1981.

right manager or wrong, went that way. They might almost have erected a guillotine at the foot of the Trinity Road stand staircase.

Of the dozen managers up to Graham Taylor, only Vic Crowe and his successor, Ron Saunders, left Villa in a better shape than they found it. Crowe's dismissal rankles with me still, for it was clear to anyone with half an eye that he was building a strong base of exceptional young players. Little, Gidman, Bobby McDonald, Steve Hunt, Gordon Cowans, John Deehan were only six of them, and it was Saunders's good fortune that he was able to inherit such riches. He made the best of it, sold every one of the half-dozen bar Cowans, and rebuilt the club by his own methods in his own name.

Saunders the enigma. This is not place to try to unravel it, either, so let us forget the bitterness and controversies, and pay tribute to the capacities of the gritty Liverpudlian who restored Villa to eminence, winning the championship and blazing the old name across the continent. His departure only emphasised his quality. Tony Barton, his assistant, held aloft the European Cup but succeeded only in underlining chairman Doug Ellis's impatience for change. The guillotine was constructed again as Barton, with a record of 11th, 6th and 10th, the European Cup and European Super Cup in his knapsack, was wheeled in tumbril to the foot of the Trinity Road stairs. Graham Turner and Billy McNeill were to follow, but just as it seemed Villa were looking over the precipice again, Graham Taylor turned up, all smiles and subtlety.

Whatever his future may hold as England manager, Taylor has performed as remarkable a job at Villa Park as he did with Watford at Vicarage Road. Perhaps his greatest feat was to separate the playing side of the club from the administrative side, making his a kingdom within a kingdom, independent in all ways within financial constraints. The players responded with dramatic, almost unbelievable, achievements.

There are those who snipe at Taylor for never having won anything substantial. But at Villa Park, anyway, it was what he created that so impressed observers, some of whom remain critical of his tactical skills. He entirely restructured the playing side, bringing in men of the highest calibre at each level, so that whatever the current defects might have been, in time there would be progressive improvement. Every manager I ever met said he had done this. Taylor actually did. In three years, the players, in terms of team spirit, good behaviour on and off the field, in taking responsibility and in judgment, were hardly recognisable from the bedraggled bunch who went down into the Second Division in 1987. In many cases, of course, they weren't, but those who remained or, in Gordon Cowans's case, returned, were immeasurably better performers by 1990.

Taylor is a manager in the proper sense of the word. He manages the organisation, methodically and astutely. Furthermore, he is lucky. I don't mean flukily so, but when planning had taken care of everything it could, luck at Aston Villa came down in his favour. In consecutive years, Villa enjoyed the full force of it, first in 1988 when they were promoted on the number of goals scored and, then the year after when the avoided relegation by about 30 Anfield minutes.

Six weeks into last season, there was talk of another long battle against relegation, even of Taylor leaving Villa Park, so grey did prospects appear. With the appointment of Dennis Booth as first-team coach, the integration of Paul McGrath as a third centre-back and the growing understanding between Cowans and David Platt, however, came a remarkable improvement. With the backbone of the team so firm, it took only a marvellous season for Tony Daley and very good ones from Nigel Spink, Ian Olney, Kent Neilsen, Derek Mountfield and others to complete the most unexpected transformation in seasons. Villa came second in the First Division and with a fraction more experience would, I am convinced, have won it. They fell away in the last dozen matches but never collapsed as so many other teams have when confronted with the Liverpool juggernaut.

Such a record only served to confirm Taylor's credentials as the new England manager. He had proved in his relationship with the Villa chairman to be clever and flexible, attributes which may be just as necessary in dealing with the Football Association as with Ellis. I hope he is also equipped to withstand any onslaught from the tabloid newspapers.

He left Villa Park a good deal more slowly than he arrived, for within a week or so of making a phone call to Ellis he was installed at Villa Park, whereas his departure took an unconscionable time. Venglos, his successor, found the club in excellent shape for the chairman's ambitious plans kept pace with the team's revival. The appointment of the former Czechoslovakian team manager ensures that Villa will be closely watched by all of football. He is ideally equipped to pioneer change at a club which did so much to shape the game itself.

In a spirit of optimism, then, let us celebrate ten outstanding players and also one of the world's best-known and long-loved clubs.

CHAPTER 2

Johnny Dixon

THIRTY-THREE YEARS AGO, A LEAN YOUNG MAN with an open smile and hair surf-waved in the style of Johnnie Ray was raised triumphantly on Villa shoulders to proclaim to Wembley 'We've won the Cup.' The fellow who modestly acknowledged the Queen's congratulations was Johnny Dixon, still such a favourite at Villa Park that when the *Sports Argus* asked readers this year to name their favourite players since war, the Geordie from Hepburn-on-Tyne came top of the poll.

The cynics who declared 'nice guys come last' forgot about Johnny Dixon who over 15 years, from a late start at 22, was the engine-room and often the engineer, too, of a Villa team struggling to revive the self-confidence of the early Thirties when Billy Walker, Eric Houghton, Pongo Waring and George Brown induced terror in First Division defences. Dixon came into a team of once-superb has-beens and left, grudgingly, as an honoured veteran giving way to younger legs.

Houghton was his manager when Villa won the Cup in 1957 which, six decades earlier, as Victoria's reign dawdled to a close, had been regarded as loaned to any other club in possession. The boardroom sideboard was said to have a permanent place for it, yet the fact was it had not been there for 37 years and hasn't since for another 33.

'I hope I'm around to see it again,' said Houghton, 80 last

Two heroes of the fifties — Dixon and Tommy Thompson.

June. 'I've had my hip replaced to get back into the team. Johnny Dixon? I'll say just this about him. He was a credit on the field and off it. He had class. The first time I saw him, I knew that. He was always energetic, and keen, a typical Geordie, gifted for playing football and mixing well with people. I don't know why the club didn't make more use of him. He should have been a club director. He was just the right type.'

Houghton and trainer Bill Moore, the man who conditioned Villa like commandos, were tense and jubilant as they watched Dixon accept the trophy on May 4 of 1957. 'It was a victory for team spirit, that,' says Houghton. 'In all my time, there never was a better. Dixon was the ideal captain. He took half the work away from me because of how he led on the field. There was a good heart under his shirt, he had a bright sense of humour and he could play a bit too. I'll say he could.'

Dixon now lives in a house crammed with the ornaments of a full life, in those couple of square miles around Walmley that are practically the dormitory suburb of Villa players past and present. He is not a voluble man, preferring action to words and to prove it was still giving an excellent account of himself at 66, for Villa All Stars this year. Now this, initially at least, was a subject worth talking about. 'We're old hands and we just play the short stuff,' he said a few days before returning to Molineux for a 10-minute-a-side charity game. 'Experienced players just move into position and the ball is pushed to them. We move gently these days.'

There was, indeed, always an air of gentility about the way Dixon played. He believed in giving everything all the time, yet he was a stylist who in his best days was almost uncontainable as an influence on Villa's behalf. He despised giving the ball away or even being caught in possession. His side knew Dixon to be the conduit through which nothing was wasted and a good deal gained, so that in those days of the W-formation with him in his favourite inside-forward position, he was always involved.

To a man, older players hate the long ball system, used not as a tactic but as a messenger of hope that one of their own forwards will be able to control the ball. Dixon condemns the practice even more strongly than most, for it is an affront to the way men played in his time, despite footwear more suited to the trenches than a football field. 'Over the last year or two there has been a lot of this stuff. It isn't my cup of tea. Only idiots waste possession. I like the old one-twos.

'In my day the wing-halves marked the inside forwards and every week you knew you would have top-class players against you. Peter Docherty, Archie Macauley, Alex Forbes, Ray Barlow, Billy Wright, and you didn't hang round to be tackled. If you didn't move the ball along you got caught and that was your look-out. It could be very painful.'

In all, Dixon played 430 times for Villa, scoring 144 goals, including one hat-trick, at Stoke on November 1, 1952, when Danny Blanchflower struck the other in a 4-1 win. Watching England as a reserve was the closest he ever came to an England cap but there was not a man in claret and blue who did not believe he should have been an international, a fate shared, ironically, with Dennis Mortimer, skipper of the European Cup-winning side.

Harry Parkes, doyen of Villa in the late Forties and also a man with claims to a place in this book, says: 'England must have had a brilliant team for Johnny not to have been picked. He was an excellent player with great ball control under pressure. He was always fair and if anyone kicked him he never retaliated. His temperament was first-class.

'It was obvious in the earliest practice matches that Johnny was going to make it. I think Ronnie Starling was his model and Ronnie was a magnificent player, a great tactician. He copied one or two of his tricks. They would both go forward, stop suddenly and pivot.'

Dixon himself pays tribute to Starling, an England international, bought for £7,500 from Sheffield Wednesday in 1937 and a Geordie not a stone of ship's coal down the Tyne at Pelaw. 'A great player was Ronnie,' he says, brown eyes alive with memories. 'I learned a lot watching him. He was my great pal and help-mate. There wasn't a lot he couldn't do with the ball.'

While the Second World War destroyed the later years of Starling's career, it delayed Dixon's entrance into the big arena. One of three children, his job as an apprentice electrical engineer kept him out of the Services and allowed him time to play for Newcastle United as an amateur for a couple of years after a few matches with Durham County Boys' team and a spell as a teenager with Spennymoor United.

Even though he appeared as a part-time pro with Newcastle for a year, it was decided at St James' Park that he could go elsewhere and Villa hurried forward to beat Everton to his signature.

'I had several practice matches behind closed doors and I made my debut against Derby in the southern section of the Football League that was introduced immediately after the war. I scored, although I don't remember a lot about it, and I also played one of the best games I remember for the Villa.'

The goal is folklore at Villa Park, for it was scored by Dixon's nose which was also battered on his last appearance at the ground when he turned his career full circle by scoring again.

He recalls: 'I went up for the ball and it bounced off my nose and landed in the net. I didn't see it because I was lying on the ground in a bit of pain. The trainer came on, pressed my nose about and I was all right.' His first was scored on April 5th, 1946. His last, on April 29th, 1961, was a far less joyous occasion, for manager Joe Mercer had brought the still-eager Dixon out of the stiffs for a final show as skipper to an admiring crowd. A Sheffield Wednesday player's elbow broke his nose but this wasn't enough to stop him demonstrating many of the finer arts he had learned with Villa.

Twenty minutes from time, Dixon chased Alan Deakin's pass into the penalty area, beating two defenders to the ball and sliding it past Ron Springett with ease.

The *Birmingham Mail* reported: 'From start to finish this was Dixon's match, and how the crowd loved it. Most of them must have gone home hoarse from all the shouting and cheering.

'They cheered like mad when they saw that Dixon had been given the honour of skippering the Villa side in his last match.

'They went almost crazy when the popular Geordie scored after 70 minutes. Hundreds of boys swarmed on to the pitch to mob Dixon, and the stands rattled as the fans stamped their feet with joy.

'Shortly afterwards he broke his nose when he was caught by a Sheffield player's elbow, but he was off only a few minutes and the crowd roared virtually every time he touched the ball.

'But it wasn't merely that the Villa fans wanted to pay tribute to a loyal clubman . . . to "Dixon of Villa Park". The simple fact was that Johnny played better than most Villa inside forwards have this season. In fact, he was the sort of man Villa have been looking for all season.

A hair-raising
moment for
Dixon.

'His distribution was first-class and he quickly set up a good understanding with Gerry Hitchens. He was dangerous in the air and cracked in several powerful shots.

'No wonder the fans were groaning after the match . . . "If only he were a little younger!"'

No wonder, too, Dixon himself left with ambivalent feelings, for he was shunted into the back-room to look after the Villa youngsters when he felt he was still equipped for League football. Today, he realises that had been the moment to strike out from Villa, to go elsewhere and perhaps return, not to enter middle-age as part of the furniture.

But he will never regret the many happy days since he, with brother Ernie as his companion, caught the train from Newcastle to New Street to become a full-time professional with one of the most famous clubs in the land. They took temporary lodgings at the Holte Hotel, a goal-kick from Villa Park, and Ernie, too, was to remain in Birmingham the rest of his working life.

Thirsty for the national game — not to mention their national obsession — the fans thronged the shabby stadiums in their drab clothing bought on ration cards. How they needed the colour and vibrant excitement of football, the working-class heroes and the identity they gave them!

Villa fielded men who had been pre-war idols, along with those on whom judgements could only be based after a season in the sectionalised competition of 1945-46. When the first whistles blew to re-start the Football League on August 31st, 1946, Frank Broome, in his one and only post-war game, centre-forward George Edwards, scorer of 39 goals in 35 games in the Football League (South), and legendary balding full backs, George Cummings and Ernie 'Mush' Callaghan, were lined up with newcomers Parkes, Les Smith, Vic Potts and Eddie Lowe, among others. The resumption was inauspicious, Villa losing 1-0 to Middlesbrough in front of 50,572 spectators. Fifteen thousand fewer turned up for the next match, also at home, and again Villa lost 1-0, this time to Everton. Dixon then scored his first League goal in a 2-1 win at Derby and, in a rather unusual reversion to the usual practice, Villa won again away, 2-1 against Wolves, before being beaten at home by Arsenal.

Dixon missed the latter two games, scored twice against Charlton in mid-October but, in and out of the team until the end of the season, failed to add another until April 4th. His attitude to scoring was simple. 'I didn't care how they went in — they all counted. I never professed to be two-footed, my right foot was better although I could do a fair job with the left. I made the most of my ability and, like most inside forwards, I worked very hard. I regarded people who didn't train as idiots, and I still do.

'Good players try to find space and if they use their brains and run intelligently they find it. I always moved round looking for the ball. As I say, I preferred inside-right but I quite enjoyed centre-forward; it wasn't a difficult job doing the same kind of things as an inside-forward, only further up the field. I can't say I liked being a winger, particularly.'

Alex Massie, Scotland's skipper in 1935, had been appointed manager in September, a post he held for five years, during which time Villa were eighth, sixth, tenth and twelfth in the First Division before a slump in 1950-51 lost him his job to George Martin, another Scot. Massie's Cup record was wretched, Villa failing to advance beyond the fourth round and actually reaching that modest place only once. His one area of success was in buying, for Trevor Ford, Dicky Dorsett, Leslie Smith, Colin Gibson and Con Martin all served Villa well.

Ford was a formidable weapon who was a good deal more popular with the fans than with his team-mates. Dixon's way of conveying this is to answer questions with a tight-lipped silence.

'Ford, what was he like?' — no answer.

Then, later . . .

'Danny Blanchflower, what do you think of him?' no answer.

The Villa players had split opinions about Blanchflower the man who became a byword for subtle, lordly football during the push-and-run era at White Hart Lane. By some, he was regarded as a man who wouldn't pass the hot milk for a team-mate's Weetabix, so independent-minded, not to mention arrogant, was he. To others, including Parkes, he was 'a great player with wonderful vision.' The facts support Parkes' opinion, yet even today Blanchflower's critics say he couldn't tackle, couldn't head and was slow.

This reminds me of a comment Mercer once made when we were discussing Stan Cullis, his friend from days as school lads at Ellesmere Port. 'Cullis,' he said, 'couldn't see properly, he couldn't pass accurately over ten yards, wasn't quick or a very good tackler. And he was the best centre-half I ever played against.'

Parkes is less reticent about Ford. 'He was greatly over-rated. His language was terrible as well.' Yet Ford was the post-war founder of Villa's outstanding line of short-stay centre forwards: Gerry Hitchens, Derek Dougan, Tony Hateley, Andy Gray and Peter Withe.

Among Massie's signings, however, the most remarkable must have been 'Con' Martin, christened Joe Cornelius Martin. A Dublin man who turned out for Drumcondra and Glentoran before the amazing Major Frank Buckley, a genius among managers, transformed him into one of the best centre-halves in England. It was for this role that Massie signed him from Buckley at Leeds United but Martin was also a first-class goalkeeper who started the 1951-52 season as a left-back and then played 26 games as goalkeeper! 'I enjoyed the job,' he said at the time. 'It wasn't all that difficult, especially if you had some hefty defenders to help you out.' Dixon says: 'He was extremely useful there and also an outstanding centre-half.'

In the 1948-49 season that Martin joined Villa, Dixon was to continue belatedly to acquire the experience of which he had been robbed by the war. Finally, he made a regular place his own after Villa had replied to a 4-0 Christmas Day drubbing by Wolves at Molineux by dishing out one themselves, 5-1 — Ford four — when Wolves went to Villa Park two days later. More than 100,000 people watched those matches and the Villa attendances in this period bear repeating. During a winter that froze football almost to a standstill for six weeks, an army of helpers managed to make Villa Park fit for play and on January 22nd 64,190 people turned up for a 1-0 victory over Arsenal. Their next home match was on February 19 and this time 68,354 saw Dixon and Ford score in a 2-1 win. The average home attendance for the season was 47,168, reflecting to a degree the turnaround in Villa's form.

Season after season they would struggle up to Christmas and then, almost as if Santa Claus had presented them with fresh motivation, climb to a respectable place in the First Division. Dixon has no real idea why, except possibly that the team was always fit. Of their final 17 matches that season. Villa won 10, drew 6 and lost only one.

Seven goals in the final 11 games of 1949-50 confirmed that Dixon could be a scorer as well as a creator. On the other hand, Villa were slipping inexorably towards the lower reaches of the division under Massie. A seven-goal humiliation at Old Trafford was a portent of the trouble that awaited them a year later. Indeed, it was exactly 12 months later that a 2-1 defeat at Highbury on March 10 — their fifth consecutive defeat — stranded Villa at the bottom of the table.

Massie had been dismissed in December, 1950, and whatever George Martin's later failings, he made the right decisions as crisis settled over Villa Park. After acquiring Blanchflower from Barnsley for £15,000, he selected the same team for the last nine matches of which six were won and three drawn. Now at last Villa had scorers to be feared: Dave Walsh, signed for £25,000 from West Brom, and Tommy 'Toucher' Thompson, another Geordie from Newcastle United, to whom Villa paid £12,000.

Dixon, leading scorer with 15 goals, remembers the time: 'We went to Wolves on March 26 seriously wondering whether we could escape. Yet we beat them at Molineux and did so again at Villa Park on the Easter Monday two days later.

'Everything had been against us. Perhaps the fact that it was a "derby" game made us pull out that indefinable extra bit. Perhaps we said to ourselves: 'Well, even if we go down, these are two games we are not going to lose.

'All I know is that we were a different side after those wins. Everything changed — luck, confidence, form. I have heard it said that Blanchflower's arrival two games before the Wolves match in 1951 turned the scales, but I don't think recovery could be put down to the influence of one man.'

Much as Blanchflower was important, the Thomspon-Dixon partnership became even more so. The Geordie connection set the goals flowing, the ever-present Dixon striking 28 in 1951-52, although it was his team-mate, 13 for the season, who won an England cap, against Wales. 'We worked well together,' says Dixon, dispassionate as ever.

Parkes, also an ever-present, is more forthcoming: 'They were superb together. "Toucher" had a lot of early pace. It's this that counts, the first ten yards, not over 40. He played a bit in front of Johnny and eventually scored more goals.'

Dixon missed eight matches with an ankle injury soon after the start of next season but it was typical of his ability to make an immediate impression that, drafted back into the side earlier than had been expected, he scored the only hat-trick of his career. The match was at Stoke and Villa won 4-1. 'I couldn't kick properly,' he says. 'Each time I hit the ball a pain shot up my leg. The performance earned a call-up to the England party for the match against Wales at Wembley.

'I just sat and watched. When you get that far and you aren't picked you're bound to wonder how well you could have done. I thought there would be another day but it wasn't to be,' he adds.

Houghton's view is: 'Of course he should have played for England. There have been many worse who have.'

Maybe a spot of flamboyance would have attracted the right sort of attention, for at grounds throughout the First Division Dixon had a reputation as the unobtrusive man who, with the highly-visible Blanchflower, made the team tick. The Irish extrovert and the Geordie introvert were, not surprisingly, on a different wavelength, the one whose personality demanded the crowd's acclaim, the other its admiration.

The joke was that Billy Goffin and Larry Canning were men-about-town compared with Dixon. One writer said at the

Wembley 1957 and a kiss he cannot forget. The captain celebrates his most memorable match.

time: 'Johnny is a teetotaller and non-smoker and not merely because he is saving up with the idea of venturing into business of his own in due course. When he has a drinking orgy it is on lemonade and he is suspected of excesses at gobbling jellies, ice cream and chocolate biscuits.'

Houghton himself took over the manager's chair the season after, and within two years Blanchflower, Thompson and Walsh were gone. Blanchflower to greatness with Spurs, Thompson to play alongside Tom Finney at Preston and, later, Stanley Matthews at Stoke, and Walsh to Walsall. The replacements were not necessarily of the same class, with the exception of Peter McParland who, even so, took more than three seasons to make serious headway. This left Dixon with the burden of providing inspiration to a forward line of average vintage.

The Cup could be Villa's only route to the record books and there did not appear to be great prospects of a lengthy run towards Wembley at a club which suffered the reputation of playing 43 games a season, 42 in League and one in the Cup.

In 1954-55, they did rather better than this, but seven matches which in many circumstances have been enough to take a team to Wembley, merely brought Villa to a fourth-round exit. It took them two matches to dispense with Brighton, of the Third Division South, and five to lose to Doncaster Rovers, whose position near the foot of the Second Division belied their willingness to defy their elite rivals through a series of draws that ended with a 3-1 victory at, of all places, The Hawthorns. Imagine the Baggies' glee at that. Dixon played at centre-forward in six of those ties, but scored only once — in the 1-3 Doncaster defeat.

From sixth place in 1955, Villa declined wretchedly the year after. Dixon was not only making goals, he was scoring most of them, too: 18 in a season that rendered only 56 altogether.

Villa went into the last match of the season needing to win. 45,120 people turned up on April 28 to watch what might have been the last rites of Villa in the First Division. It was a malign coincidence that the opposition were Albion. Winger Les Smith, signed from Wolves only six weeks previously, never scored two more valuable goals and these, plus a Len Millard own goal, assured Villa of safety by fractions of a goal, Huddersfield going down instead.

By then, Houghton had made another acquisition: trainer Bill Moore. Villa were an efficient side whose product improved in direct proportion to the heaviness of the ground and the lateness of the season. Nor was Dixon any longer the lone midfield provider, for Houghton had bought Jackie Sewell for £20,000 from Sheffield Wednesday, £14,500 less than Wednesday had paid four years earlier when the Cumberland man had become the most expensive purchase in League history. Wing-halves Pat Saward and Stan Crowther gave an element of abrasiveness to the midfield while Jimmy Dugdale, Stan Lynn and Peter Aldis, in front of goalkeeper Nigel Sims, formed one of the tightest defences in the First Division. If ever there were a team designed for a knockout competition, this was it.

Dixon captained this happy blend of super-fit men. He says: 'Winning the Cup was due to our condition and the team spirit. We started to find our form after Christmas and got more and more confident. Everyone wanted the ball and when we beat Burnley that was an omen. We were never able even to draw at Turf Moor when we played well. It was one of these things, so that when we managed a 1-1 draw in the sixth-round tie there, we knew we could beat them at Villa Park.

'In the semi-final we were always behind to Albion at Molineux but McParland scored twice and we drew again. There's no doubt we were lucky to beat them by a Billy Myerscough goal at St Andrew's.'

And so it was on to Wembley. Dixon took with him a foot-long elephant hair, sent to him as a lucky omen by a supporter in Northern Rhodesia when it looked as if Villa might be relegated the season before.

Before the kick-off, trainer Moore took him aside to say: 'I've told Stan Lynn and Nigel Sims to stick close to you, so that when we've won the cup, they can carry you on their shoulders.' This confidence was not shared by the bookmakers who made the 'Busby Babes' clear favourites. And why not? League champions by a margin of eight points, man-for-man this young team appeared far superior: only McParland of the Villa team would, I think, have been certain of a place in it.

We know, however, that football, like life, is not so simple, or there would be no such trade as bookmaking. United were beaten in a match of vivid controversy which I deal with elsewhere.

Dixon's memories are unleashed as he pours forth: 'It was the happiest day of my life — that wonderful day, May 4, 1957, when Villa won the Cup for the seventh time. For 13 years I had been at Villa Park without winning a thing. The previous season we had missed relegation by a decimal point. Yet there I was — captain of the Cup-winning side.

'When I made the pre-match introductions to the Duke of Edinburgh, I described both Stan Lynn and Peter Aldis as right-backs. I realised my slip, but I was quite surprised when the Duke said: "You seem to have a lot of right-backs in your team."

'With about ten minutes to go Les Smith was injured and when he was being treated, I suddenly realised we were going to win. The Queen would soon be handing me the Cup. I was so overcome with emotion, I nearly burst into tears there and then.'

He accepts that the injury to goalkeeper Ray Wood might have been the decisive incident of the match. 'Peter McParland was not a dirty or a nasty player and it was perfectly legal to charge a 'keeper in those days. Wood tried to shield himself but unfortunately he didn't shield his jaw from the collision. It was a pity it happened but it takes no credit from our win. These days, of course, you aren't allowed to touch a goal-keeper. Things have become farcical. A chap goes down if he's so much as touched. Then he waves everyone upfield and kicks the ball straight to the opposition.'

Sadly, the remainder of Dixon's career with Villa was an anti-climax. An allergy to penicillin that brought him out in bumps, followed by a serious bout of influenza and then a cartilage operation spoiled the following season, in which he played only 14 games.

Houghton was replaced by Joe Mercer the year afterwards and mention of Mercer meets one of Dixon's silences. Only one game from another Cup final on March 14th, Villa went to The Hawthorns six weeks later again requiring two points to stay in the First Division. The victory of three years before proved only to be a reprieve, for Villa drew and were relegated.

Supporters' player of the year in 1958-59, Dixon was given just four games the year after as Mercer's team headed back to the top flight as champions. He remains indignant about this about his demotion to the reserves and, as time went by, to the third team. Then two days before the last of the 1960-61 season Mercer called him into his office to ask him whether he was going to retire. 'The next thing he called up the papers to tell them I was finishing,' he says.

This is always a difficult time for a manager, especally when the player has been such an invaluable and loyal servant as Dixon who, despite the occasional story that he might be going to Portsmouth, Grimsby or Walsall was a Lion, tooth and claw. Clearly Mercer tried to make Dixon's a memorable send-off and so it turned out to be.

But Dixon regrets accepting the offer to coach the third team even if the fans were content that he should remain a Villa man. 'I have always been lucky with the fans,' he says. 'Although I had "the bird" a few times it was never bad. I am very grateful to them.'

The gratitude was shared. Dixon stayed six further years and then he and his wife, Brenda, bought an ironmonger's store that also sold fancy goods. This was most inappropriate. There was nothing fancy about Johnny Dixon, he was the plain man's guide to team football.

Johnny Dixon

Born Hepburn-on-Tyne, Co. Durham, 10th December 1923. League appearances 392, goals 132. F.A. Cup 38 appearances, 12 goals: Total 430/144. F.A. Cup-winners medal 1957. Winner Villa Terrace Trophy 1959. Other club: Newcastle United part-time pro.

CHAPTER 3

Stan Lynn

REPORTERS, SEARCHING HEAVEN AND EARTH for a new superlative to describe the power of Stan Lynn's shot, were quick to alight on the first Soviet Union satellite for comparison. On October 4, 1957, the Sputnik was launched to the wonderment of the world and the surprise of the USA where it was complacently believed that space was their domain.

'Sputnik Stan' never really caught on among the down-to-earth Holte Enders whose admiration for the feriocious power of the right back's kicking did not extend to dodgy alliteration. They preferred the simple, evocative 'Stan the Wham', and even today the nickname is greeted with immediate recognition at either Villa Park or St Andrew's. Lynn played for both clubs, you see, rebuilding a career with Birmingham City at the unlikely age of 33.

There are many veteran supporters at both who will insist that no player struck a ball harder than the lad from Bolton who was signed, raw and bristling with competitiveness, from Accrington Stanley. His right-foot shot was of a velocity to induce thoughts of ultimate weapons or direction-finding meteors. It wasn't only in charity football, from which the now 62-year-old Lynn has only just retired, that the fear-factor came into play. Fans jammed between the laundry wall and the goal-line at Fellows Park watched in awe as a penalty floored the Walsall goalkeeper. It is sworn that a railway train driver, watching from a nearby track, nearly choked on his 'piece' when he saw that.

At his home in Shirley, Lynn remembers another instance: 'The balls in those days became very heavy, like sandbags, and I drove a penalty that knocked the Cardiff goalkeeper backwards into the net. The trainer was called on to bring him round.'

How he loved the flourish of penalty-taking, too. He is as happy as ever to boast that he prayed the 1957 F.A. Cup final with Manchester United would be a draw so he could be called on to take a last-minute penalty. 'Oh, yes,' he says. 'The idea was thrilling. I suppose I missed three or four in my entire career and, by the way, they weren't all blasted. I fooled quite a few goalkeepers by sidefooting the ball past them.'

Lynn regards himself as too much of a footballer for the taste of two managers, especially that of the late Joe Mercer who sold him to Blues for the £10,000 he cost Villa, but the common view is different. From the day he arrived at Villa Park, parting as straight as the Fosse Way down the centre of two Brylcreem-slicked portions of hair, Lynn had a reputation for fearlessness and vigorous tackling.

Yet the appearance was deceptive. In his whole career, Lynn was booked but once and although players during his 15 years — from 1951 to 1966 — were allowed far more licence, his was not a record to chill the heart. His solitary caution was against a fellow Lancastrian, a man whom Lynn regards as the outstanding footballer of the age, Tom Finney. And, incidentally, Lynn still believes he was innocent.

'It was in the first minute and I was just letting Tom know I was around, like every half-decent full back does. Amazingly, this referee came from Horwich where I had lived and he was also a friend of my wife's family. I refused to give him a lift home after that, I can tell you.

'Tom was a great player, as I said. He was a natural in any position in the forward line and, because of that alone, I think

Lynn happy at
Villa in 1960.

he was more effective than Stan Matthews. I have no doubt
about whom I would nominate as the best, though — Duncan
Edwards of Manchester United. What a tragedy! His death
after the Munich air crash lost us the best player I every saw,
and that even includes John Charles who has to be second.
Edwards's every touch spoke of quality. A nice guy, too.'

Lynn came from a working-class Bolton family who, like
everyone else in the cotton towns of those days, were daft
about football. His own work in a cotton mill was called 'a
control of engagement' job and kept him from being
conscripted into national service. It also stopped him signing
forms as a professional footballer.

Before this, however, he had almost give up the game. As
a shrimp of a right-winger with Whitecroft Road Secondary

Modern School, he dazzled everyone but the league scouts. Maybe they thought the 5ft 3ins lad you could thread through the eye of a needle hadn't the build for the hurly-burly of high-grade football. Anyway, Lynn gave up for a year in sheer disappointment and went into a nearby mill as an apprentice stripper and grinder.

Crowds might never have witnessed Lynn's right-footed demolition work had not Bill Whitworth persuaded him that a few matches in one of his three Bolton Boys Federation teams would brighten up the drudgery of mill life. Shortly afterwards, he was moved from the wing when a right-back failed to turn up and, although he did not like the position at first, there was no escaping his fate. Or his dad.

He says: 'My father who, I'm told, was just about the toughest wing-half ever seen in Bolton football, came to see me from time to time at right back and he used to play hell with me for not getting stuck in. I was small and a bit timid; in fact, I don't mind admitting it, I was a bit scared. But my father kept drumming it into me — "You'll get hurt if you don't go in hard." I never forgot that and when I grew up I followed his advice to the letter.'

Matthews, Finney and Harry Burrows are three who would vouch for that. Lynn always tried a spot of psychology on the legendery Matthews, a man whose willingness to discuss injuries and ailments might be thought to border on hypochondria, except that even the most elusive winger who ever wriggled his hips in front of a desperate full back could expect to be caught with a reinforced leather toe cap at least once a match.

Lynn says: 'I always asked him about his latest knock and he'd tell me that, for instance, his ankle was playing up. "Right, Stan," I'd put in, "you'd better keep it away from me because I'll be having a go at it."

'Then I would always have a pre-match chat with Harry Burrows. I'd put my arm around Harry and say: "You see those empty seats, Harry lad, which one do you want me to put you in?" I always had a good game against Harry.

About to release
something
frightening.

'Generally, I used to have good games against the big names. They used to inspire me. I loved it. I suppose the two who gave me most problems were Frank Blunstone, of Chelsea, and Billy Rudd, of Manchester City. Four times I think I played against Rudd and not once did I master him. Blunstone was different but he always had me in a spot of bother away from Villa Park.'

His formidable reputation was years ahead of him as he began to fill out of Whitworth's. Soon Accrington Stanley became interested in him, more as a winger than a back, and so it was that he found himself on the right flank in his first match for the Division Three (North) team. 'There was no elastic in the knicks they gave me,' he says, 'and I had to run around holding them up with one hand. I was too shy to shout to the touchline for tape.'

Life for Accrington was hand-to-mouth in an area which was still the forcing house of English football, numbering half-a-dozen First Division teams of high achievement. In Lowry-land, the footballers were anything but stiff, formal and muffled figures on an industrial landscape. They were the everyday heroes of Bolton and Preston, Blackburn and Burnley, the Lofthouses, Claytons, Finneys and McIlroys, all regular international players of renown.

Stanley, founder members of the Football League, were to become the victims, almost the sacrificial victims, of the decline of cotton, for in 1962, after years of 'chipping in' by directors, they folded. Even in Lynn's time, they struggled on a staff of 14 professionals and a bunch of part-timers, of whom he was one, paid a sum of £3-a-match. Existence was always temporarily eased by the sale of a player and when Villa, in the person of George Cummings, began to turn up regularly to study the young and now sturdier 5ft 11ins Lynn, financial relief was in the air.

Cummings, a chip of granite and a Scots international who had retired as a player only a year previously, watched Lynn three or four times and despite his often-repeated verdict that his only doubt was the way Lynn kicked a ball, recommended him to George Martin, the Villa manager. 'Cummings must have been one of the greatest full backs ever,' says Lynn. 'His criticism was that I hit the ball with the outside of my foot and he would sometimes tell me that if only I struck it properly I would play for England.

'I had no idea Villa wanted to sign me. There was a telegram from someone — I didn't know who — to Accrington telling me to meet him at Bury. It turned out to be Martin. I had never even been to Birmingham but it was my chance and I

Stan Lynn soon after arriving in Birmingham in pin-stripe suit, hair carved with a parting.

took it. I was 22 at the time and the club set me up in digs at Perry Barr with a bloke called Jack Hindle, who had been signed from Barrow, and a Cockney called Bill Simpson.

'I was absolutely dedicated to fitness, always was. I never took a drop to drink until we won the Cup final, and although I went out with the lads, I stuck to orange juice and I didn't smoke either. I had 21 years of job satisfaction and it was worth it. I see these players who finish early and I often wonder how long they would have lasted if they had led the lives of proper professionals.'

In his first season, 1950-51, with Villa, Lynn made nine first-team appearances, his debut at left back at Huddersfield where 25,093 people watched the home side win 4-2. More notable even than Lynn's debut was the final Villa match for Trevor Ford and, incidentally, one of the last for George Edwards, another goalscorer of eternal Villa fame. These were days of transition, when players, often robbed of six years' football by the Second World War, were being replaced by boys who had sheltered with their families from the Luftwaffe's bombs. The old order, among whom Edwards had an honourable place, were, sadly, never to fulfil themselves completely.

'I was put in at left back on my debut and I was no lover of that,' says Lynn. He had to wait from October 14 to December 23 for his next game, this time serving as centre forward before Martin signed Dave Walsh, a specialist. Lynn actually scored that time and, when Irishman Walsh was signed for £25,000 from West Brom, was rewarded with a move to right back, the dependable Harry Parkes swopping to the left. This state of affairs lasted two matches, during which Lynn scored his first Villa penalty goal — against Fulham in a 3-0 home victory — before finding himself labelled 'a utility man' and making just three more appearances before the end of the season in which Villa finished 15th.

'I came from Accrington as a penalty taker,' he says. 'We were given one against Fulham and everyone seemed a bit dubious about taking it, so I offered. I loved it. I scored with another against Arsenal that season on the afternoon Peter Aldis made his debut.' The couple were to form a full-back partnership that is remembered to this day but, in the short term, Aldis's inclusion at left back meant there was no place for Lynn.

Fashions changed and Lynn welcomes a £1,000 loyalty cheque from Villa as Gerry Hitchens and Peter McParland congratulate him on his luck.

Together, these two men were to total more than 600 appearances for Villa, Lynn 323 of them, but while Aldis managed just one goal, Lynn struck 38. That Aldis goal, when it came in a September, 1952 match against Sunderland, was as spectacular as it was unique. The former Cadbury chocolate maker, once a centre forward with Pineapple School, scored from 35 yards with, believe it or not, a header. Even Lynn's boyhood idol, Tommy Lawton, the man on whom he modelled the Grand Canyon hair style, never managed that.

The next was a sound decision for Villa who finished sixth in the First Division. Johnny Dixon scored 28 times and Lynn only once, when Martin, concerned at a loss of form that brought six defeats in seven games, selected him on November 17 in a despairing bid for goals. Lynn duly supplied one in a 2-2 draw, and it is typical of the fortunes of football that Aldis suffered a serious cartilage injury, necessitating a swop by Parkes to left back and 24 consecutive games at right back for Lynn. Oddly, in that entire season, Villa did not score from a penalty. He can't remember when it was he missed one against West Brom but a picture on his dentist's wall reminds him to this day of the fact that he did fail from 12 yards against Villa's Black Country rivals, as if the pain of having teeth extracted were not sufficient to be going on with.

Martin evidently preferred the Parkes-Aldis duo at this stage, for, when Aldis was available, Lynn inevitably lost out. 1952-53 was a patchy season for Villa, despite players of the quality of Danny Blanchflower, Parkes, Tommy Thompson and Walsh providing a certain style.

Lynn fared even worse initially when Eric Houghton returned to the club he adored to take over from Martin. Yet this was an important year for him because he was introduced to Bill Moore's parade-ground methods of training. 'Eric was smashing, perhaps a bit soft, while Bill was fantastic,' he says. 'I always loved training as much as the game. Playing was just a bonus to me. In those days, discipline wasn't as strict as today — at least it wasn't unless Bill was around. If anyone arrived a minute later for training, he'd tell him not to bother to change; you could come back for a 2 o'clock session instead. The seasons he was there were the fittest of my career.'

Houghton's record as Villa manager was not particularly auspicious until they won the F.A. Cup in 1956-57. His first full season was creditable but Villa escaped relegation in 1955-56 by a fraction of a goal by winning their final match 3-0 at home to West Brom. Yet the improvement in Peter McParland, the purchase of Jackie Sewell from Sheffield Wednesday for £20,000, and the backing of such players as goalkeeper Nigel Sims, Aldis and Lynn, Stan Crowther, bought to replace Blanchflower who had been sold to Spurs, Pat Saward and Les Smith, offered promise. Probably most important, however, was the securing of Jimmy Dugdale from

West Bromwich, and the consequent increased stability at the heart of the defence.

Scoring League goals was a problem in the season Villa won the Cup for the seventh time, a record equalled only by Spurs. But McParland embarked on a devastating run in the later rounds, scoring six times in five ties, including two in the Wembley final victory which was clouded by controversy.

Lynn, at last a consistent first-team player, says: 'In that year the conditions at Villa Park were terrible. The mud was the worst I've ever seen. It made our fitness tell. Right from the beginning, we somehow knew we were going to win the Cup. We never even thought we would get beaten. It happens with a lot of winners. If your name is on it, then that's it.

'We had two terrific semi-finals with West Brom. We needed Peter Mac to score four minutes from the end of the first at Molineux and then Billy Myerscough scored the winner at St Andrews. I had a bit of luck there. Ronnie Allen's shot was bound for goal when the ball hit my heel and looped over the bar. I boasted afterwards that it was deliberate!

'Why did we get to Wembley? Simple, it wasn't skill, it was fitness.'

United had a magnificent young team — the Busby Babes, soon so tragically to be destroyed by the Munich disaster — that included Duncan Edwards, Tommy Taylor, Bobby Charlton, Eddie Colman, Roger Byrne: there was hardly a name that does not ring down the years with vibrant promise. Two weeks before the May 4 final, United had been on the brink of a breathtaking hat-trick of major trophies, the European Cup, the F.A. Cup and the First Division championship. Real had removed them from the European semi-final and Villa were to end hopes of a Double, last achieved by themselves 60 years earlier.

The decisive moment occurred early on. McParland, chasing a through ball, collided heavily with United goalkeeper Ray Wood who slumped to the thick green turf clutching the ball as if it were a wounded child. Wood was lifted from turf, concussed, and on to a stretcher as United fans jeered the Villa left-winger, at best for a misjudgment cause by over-enthusiasm, at worst for a malicious deed.

There can be little doubt that today, under sterner justice, McParland would have been booked, maybe even sent off, and the fact that referee Coultas awarded a United free kick implied that he considered the Irishman guilty of an offence. Coultas said later: 'It was not a malicious foul. McParland did not try to harm Wood. He was just a bit robust, as they call it. Just a bit too enthusiastic in playing the British game of getting stuck in.'

Others were not so understanding and, certainly, Villa players to this day will admit that United were disrupted by what turned out to be a fractured cheekbone to Wood which meant that the manager Matt Busby could not risk using his goalkeeper as more than a nuisance on the wing until, in a desperate move to save the game, he was returned to goal with eight minutes to go.

In the meantime, McParland had scored twice. The Irishman studiously headed in Johnny Dixon's cross past replacement goalkeeper Jackie Blanchflower for the first, and five minutes later Billy Myerscough — controversially chosen instead of Derek Pace — struck the bar, leaving McParland to add a second.

United had little liking for Villa's strong tackling or their non-stop industry, yet when Tommy Taylor headed their goal with those eight minutes to go, the Villa fans hung on nervously before Dixon hoisted the trophy for the world to acknowledge. 'Great moments,' says Lynn. 'It was the only time I went to Wembley and I have been trying for ages to get a video of it.

'Was there any intent by Peter to hurt Wood? I don't think so. A few days earlier we had seen Gento go in to challenge Wood and he just bounced off him. You have to realise that goalkeepers weren't protected as they are now. Peter went in with typical enthusiasm and I think he hit him as Woody tried to get out of the way.'

In the newsagents shop Lynn bought practically next door to Villa Park.

Be that as it may, I still wince when I remember the lateness of McParland's thrust into the penalty area and, after some consideration, Lynn admits: 'Well, maybe it was a bit rash but it was our big day and Mac showed it. He just wanted to do well. We all used to go in hard in those days but it was the hardness of enthuisastic players. I never minded a whack so long as the other guy was prepared to take one back. Nowadays there are a lot of good actors about, and I must say most of them are not dedicated as we were, and I don't think they have as much fun either.

'There were some great lads in that team. Peter Mac was the comic and Les Smith told the jokes. Nigel Sims was half-soaked. In the run-up to the final he lost a stone in weight. Aldis was the gentleman and Johnny Dixon the miser who wouldn't spend a penny when a ha'penny would do. None of us thought we would lose against United, though.

'It wasn't the same in 1959-60 when we reached a semi-final against Wolves. I have never seen a manager as nervous as Joe Mercer was. He made a bad mistake, too. He picked Jimmy MacEwan on the wing when everyone knew he wasn't fit.'

The season after their Cup victory, Villa did not flourish as they had expected to. Nevertheless, Lynn made history. In the home match with Sunderland on January 11, he became the first full back to score a hat-trick in Division One. Neatly, he tucked two penalties past the Sunderland goalkeeper, Fraser, one to Lynn's left, the second to his right.

As if this were not sufficient humiliation, Lynn then hit the Geordies with one of the game's sucker punches. He ran in on the blind side of the winger and swung his right foot with thunderous power at Les Smith's short corner. Villa won 5-2, both sides signed the ball and presented it to him and on Monday morning a helmet was delivered to his house, proclaiming across the front 'Up the Villa'.

A note read 'Oh! Stan, we weep — Signed Ever Faithful'.

Smith and Lynn regularly used their little ploy and, in all, the season brought nine goals for the right back who missed only two games.

Lynn was to score two penalties in the defeat of Bristol City which was to ensure Villa promotion two years later, yet for all the excitement and tension of a magnificent season when Gerry Hitchens, Bobby Thomson and McParland were to score more than twenty goals each, and the ever-present Lynn seven, the full back's most memorable contribution was for those who treasure moments of divine inspiration — and maybe a little humour — more than the dry repetition of statistics.

On New Year's Eve, 1955, Lynn set off 60 yards from goal scarcely knowing where he was heading, except that it was in the general direction of Huddersfield Town's goal. On and on he went, to the incredulity of trainer Bill Moore. 'I know I haven't been in the game as long as many people,' said Moore at the time. 'But I still reckon it was the most amazing goal I have ever seen.' Yes, Lynn scored, challenged only by one man, centre-half Ken Taylor, before executing a sweet little dummy-pass and slipping the ball past goalkeeper Jack Wheeler.

'That's the way to do it,' a grinning Lynn is reported to have boasted to Huddersfield's Davie Hickson. With few arguments, it was also described as the Goal of the Year.

For all this, Villa were an unprepossessing side in the later years of the Fifties. No-one who follows them will be surprised that failings in '58-59 brought demands from the Shareholders' Association for the replacement of directors Joe Broughton and Bruce Normansell who were held partly responsible for the club's lack of ambition compared with their neighbours. It was as true then as it always has been that a football club is only as strong as the team on the field and, while the directors' seats were indented by the same bottoms, by December the manager's wasn't. Out went Houghton, in came Mercer from Sheffield United.

The following year Villa were relegated. Lynn's relationship with the new manager, Mercer, was always uneasy. He had been dropped from the F.A. Cup semi-final against Forest which Villa lost 0-1 at Hillsborough but was called up for the last two matches of the season, the climax — or anti-climax — coming a few miles down the A41 at The Hawthorns.

'That was the most shattering experience of my football career,' says Lynn, wincing at the memory. 'We knew we had to win to stay up. Hitchens gave us the lead on a wet and slippery night and we had high hopes. Then Ronnie Allen equalised with a soft goal, hitting the ball with his shin. We were sick, I can tell you, and an end-of-the-season 'do' had been arranged for us at The Tower in Edgbaston. It was like a funeral.

'Joe had some funny ideas and I knew that he might want to get rid of me. I was determined to get my place back and I did.'

Mercer had his say at the time, for Villa fans were puzzled as to why one of the favourite characters so often found himself in the Central League side. 'I expected a man with Stan's spirit to "have a go",' said the future England manager, 'but just how hard he has trained and fought back to get into the side has been a revelation to me.

'It is a professional effort on his part. We could do nothing except to tell him what we wanted. Having been told, he stuck his toes in and produced it. He has proved me wrong and I am delighted he has done it.' And thus, the craggy Lynn was unleashed on Second Division left wingers. He and Villa prospered through a season that brought them the Division Two title. 'That season was the highlight of my career,' says Lynn.

It featured a match which middle-aged Villa fans still talk of with a catch in their voice. On March 30, 1960, Liverpool established a four-goal lead that had the home fans wondering whether the promotion prossibility was just a myth. In the next 19 minutes, McParland, Thompson, twice, and Lynn with a penalty made it 4-4 as the Holte End trembled collectively in gleeful excitement. In those final five minutes, Lynn kicked Hunt's shot off the line and McParland skied an easy six-yard chance high over the bar.

'Unforgettable,' says Lynn. 'I remember nearly every kick. I used to say to Nigel Sims, "If you miss it I'll be on the line, and that time I was." '

Thirty then, Lynn's Villa days were coming to a close. He made only 14 First Division appearances the next season as

Lynn asleep with the Cup — no, I don't believe it either.

Mercer set about re-creating his team, and even missed a penalty in the first leg of the first League Cup final at Rotherham where Villa lost 3-0 after extra time at Villa Park. In October 1961 he was transferred to Birmingham City, much to the chagrin of Blues supporters who felt their team was acquiring not just a has-been but a Villa has-been at that.

It took them a couple of matches to change their minds, for Lynn, as ever, was a man to be considered. He played 148 times for Villa's neighbours, scored 30 more of those resounding goals and even won a League Cup tankard when Blues beat Villa in the 1963 two-legged final.

'Those were great days,' he says. 'Villa tried to give me some stick but I think I helped our tactics because I told Hellawell what to do against Charlie Aitken. He murdered him. I was the oldest man on the field.'

At 38, he left Blues and played on for a while with non-League Stourbridge. His reluctance to leave a football unpunished has never faltered. He still plays occasional charity football matches, although his preference today is to whack a golf ball in the company of old Villa colleagues on days off from the toolroom stores at a Shaftmoor Lane, Birmingham, factory.

I bet he hits it miles!

Stan Lynn

Born Bolton, Lancs, 18th June 1928. Bought for £10,000 from Accrington Stanley. Villa League appearances: 281, goals 36. F.A. Cup 36/1. FL Cup 6/1. Total 323/38. F.A. Cup winners medal 1957; Second Division championship 1960. Sold to Birmingham City, October 1961.

CHAPTER 4

Gerry Hitchens

EVEN THE IMPARTIAL TONES OF THE *SPORTS Report* score-reader occasionally rise, just perceptibly, on the syllable before he announces a score that will lift hundreds of thousands of backs from their seats.

On this occasion, November 14th, 1959, he intoned 'Aston Villa' and you knew even he, the master of deadpan, was not able to resist a small dramatic flourish to attend 'Aston Villa 11, Charlton Athletic 1' before continuing on his unfavouring way.

Five of the goals in this football massacre were scored by a young man whose fair hair had recovered from the controlled butchery of his army barber, an act just as calculated as his had been at Villa Park on that overcast day. Gerry Hitchens, of whom much had been expected since his arrival two years previously, had finally convinced a sceptical home crowd that he was not just a handsome miner's son with more dress sense than killer instinct.

A week later, he was to score three more goals at Bristol City followed by two at home to Scunthorpe, as Villa headed back to Division One leaving behind them, it now seems incredible, Liverpool. Hitchens was to score only five goals after the new year that season, yet his burst of ten in three games was to presage an impact on the First Division that is still talked of in terms of wonder wherever middle-aged Villa supporters gather.

Luton's Ron Baynham beats Hitchens to the ball.

Hitchens was born on October 8th, 1934, in Rawnsley, Staffordshire, and at 19 joined Kidderminster Harriers, from whom Cardiff City bought him for £1,500 to partner Trevor Ford, a former Villa centre-forward with the fire of the Welsh Valleys in his belly. Forty goals in 100 games for the Welsh team persuaded Villa that a sizeable investment was required and on December 20th, 1957, Hitchens was signed by Eric Houghton for £22,500.

Let Houghton take up the story: 'We had won the F.A. Cup the season before but I believed we needed a strong, young centre-forward and my chief scout, Sidney Dickinson, was insistent that Gerry Hitchens was the man. Sidney had followed him everywhere and he was so good at his job that I had to listen.

'The board of directors refused to give me the £25,000 Cardiff wanted but said they could raise half of it, so I went ahead and sold Derek Pace to Sheffield United. I was sorry to sell 'Doc'. He was a grand lad and a good player whom I had left out of the Cup final team but I raised £12,500 from United and then went back to Cardiff and offered £20,000. In the end we split the difference and Hitchens came for £22,500.'

Three years earlier, Villa had turned their back on the same young man at a price of £1,000. Now, here in a Cardiff hotel, was Houghton busy trying to sweet-talk Hitchens' fiancee, Meriel Jones, of Pontypridd, into allowing him to move from the frost-greened hills to the grimy, smoke-logged city 100 miles away. It took two hours but he succeeded. For Meriel, the move heralded a life of riches, glamour and, finally, blinding, numbing grief.

It had taken a cloak-and-beard campaign for Houghton to deliver his Christmas present to the Villa fans, with West Midland neighbours Birmingham City and Wolves also chasing the signature of a man destined to play for England.

Hitchens said: 'I know most of the lads because I played against them for the Army recently and they are a great club. I have always been at the bottom in my professional football career — with Kidderminster and Cardiff but let's hope I can help to alter that with the Villa. I hope I can help them to climb up the table.'

Twenty-four hours later, he made his debut against Birmingham, Villa losing 0-2 in front of 39,889 fans. Five days after that, on Boxing Day, 40,638 watched him score the first of 96 goals in 160 appearances for the club which, despite all of his travels, he regarded with special affection.

His first season was unspectacular, and one of the players to join Villa a season later, a man who was to play a crucial part in the burnishing of the rough-edged centre forward, Ron Wylie, provides one good reason why. 'Players on national service were always affected, whatever they said. It was difficult for them to fall into a routine, no matter how well they thought they trained away from their club,' he says.

'I'll go further and add that it was not until 18 months to two years after a player had left the services that he fulfilled his real potential. Gerry still had six months in the army when I joined Villa and the true player did not properly emerge until the season he left. By then he was a handful for any defence.'

Villa finished that 1957-58 season with a flourish,

That was close!

undefeated in their final six matches, winning four of them, Hitchens scoring four goals in the period. His four months had rendered 11 goals which made him joint second-highest scorer with Jackie Sewell on 11 goals, that Irish charger of a winger, Peter McParland, having totalled 17.

There was considerable confidence at Villa Park that the 1958-59 season would bring a considerable improvement from 14th position, yet Villa, at first under Houghton and then under Joe Mercer, were relegated. It seems amazing today that a team who included Nigel Sims, Stan Lynn, Vic Crowe, Jimmy Dugdale, Les Smith, Peter McParland, Hitchens and Wylie could amass only 30 points (two for a win, one for a draw) but they scored only 58 goals and let in 77, suffering an early 2-7 defeat against West Ham and then a 3-6 against Leicester.

The much-loved Mercer was persuaded to leave Sheffield United and take over at Villa Park in December 1958. By mid-March it seemed that his knowledge, approachable manner and tactical skill would rescue his new club from another of their regular bouts in the Second Division but, after a winning spell of three games in March, during which Hitchens in another super-abundant spell scored six goals, Villa subsided. Six games away from Villa Park — where the season's crowd average was no less than 32,837 — were too much of a burden and nine matches yielded only four points and in passing, a single goal for Hitchens. This was scored in the final match against West Bromwich Albion, which Villa needed to win to stay up. They drew 1-1 and Villa supporters still find it hard to forgive their near neighbours.

No matter what Villa's league form, the F.A. Cup has always had a dramatic effect on them. Men wearied by the weekly drudgery of draw or defeat find they have wings on their heels where football's most famous knockout competition is concerned. So it was with Villa 1959-style and a succession of surprise results, culminating in the 4-1 defeat of Everton at Goodison Park, brought Villa face to face with Nottingham Forest at Hillsborough in a semi-final. Villa, Cup winners two years earlier, went down 0-1, a defeat which, as so often happens, left the vanquished with a sense of anti-climax and irrecoverable morale.

Villa swaggered through the next season, aristocracy among the lower classes, Hitchens and McParland racing for the top goalscoring spot neck and neck, until, with six matches remaining, both suddenly stopped on a combined total of 50. Hitchens struck 23 in the League and two in the Cup, his Irish friend, 22 and three while Bobby Thomson, a wavy-haired Scot bought from Wolves, added 20 of the 89 that made their side one of the most attractive in the country.

Wylie remembers that before the 11-1 victory over Charlton, Mercer, concerned at the shortage of goals — they had scored 29 in 17 games, six to Hitchens — called the centre-forwards, Wylie and Thomson, into his office and told each of them that if they did not score more often he would be out of the team. 'I told him I never scored so I wasn't part of the argument,' says Wylie.

Unmarked, Hitchens rises above it all — but this header went over.

Some players are born to score goals, some have goalscoring thrust upon them — Hitchens was in the second category of this paraphrase and, indeed, the magic was at times mystifyingly slow to work its spell on him. Only a fortnight before the tireless forward's five goals, a Birmingham football paper had carried what amounted to a warning notice. The *Blue Mail* noted that 20-year-old Ken Price was challenging Hitchens, then 24, in a Battle of the Villa Park centre-forwards.

'It won't be for lack of trying if Hitchens isn't helping with that net-filling,' the report said. 'But the trouble with Gerry is . . . he's unorthodox. At the same time the big asset of Gerry is . . . he's unorthodox.'

'His hard, galloping style — it's earned him the sometime nickname from his team-mates of ''Champion the Wonder

Horse''. His awkward but effective ball-control. His amazing ability to beat a man the ''wrong'' way, after landing himself in an impossible position. It all means that many a centre half is left wondering how Hitchens will play his football next. Which is good for Villa. Good for Gerry. But not yet good for enough goals to claim first place against all-comers. And the one ''all-comer'' to watch is Mr (rapidly) Rising Price.'

The diagnosis of Hitchens may have been correct, the forecast was wider than a left back's right-footed shot. Ken Price never wore claret and blue for the first team and a sceptical observer may feel that this piece of journalism was designed to motivate Hitchens the tiny fraction that is the difference between hope and fulfilment.

Hitchens was no longer a Lance Corporal and expectations had consequently risen within the club that he would provide the strength to set alongside McParland's power, Thompson's effervescence and Wylie's guile. By then, too, yet another Scot, Jimmy MacEwan, had joined Villa to provide speed and tricks down the right side. MacEwan, Thomson, Hitchens, Wylie and McParland may not have been the best forward line to have brought the Holte End to its toes but it still has a dangerous ring to it.

'What Price this Villa attack now!' read the Saturday-night headline, adding: 'Gerry Hitchens slammed his critics today in the best possible way — with five golden goals in this deep humiliation of Charlton'.

His first goal in a month took two minutes, the centre-forward running in Thomson's shot that had rebounded off Willy Duff. Although Charlton equalised, Thomson scored the first of his two and then, after 29 minutes, Hitchens prodded his second, waiting only 11 minutes to complete his hat-trick. This was a typical Hitchens goal, made up in parts of persistence, coolness and skill, for two defenders appeared to have time to move the ball away but delayed for a fateful instant which to a goalscorer amounts to a bargain offer. For weeks Hitchens had suffered the anguish of the man for whom

Never a man to give up a race.

everything is nearly right, now the needle had found the groove and the suffering was for someone else.

Mercer had forecast: 'One of these days we will be filling somebody's net' and the three-goal lead was increased to four a minute after half-time when, taking goalkeeper Nigel Sims's clearance 40 yards from goal, he rounded a defender and beat Duff again. He did so for the fifth time on the hour, a raking, angled drive leaving the goalkeeper on the ground clutching his arm and possibly his reputation, too. Duff left the field at this point and it was almost as if Hitchens took pity on the opposition, for he failed to score another.

Wylie recalls Hitchens as 'a gentleman. A really nice fella who knew how to handle himself properly on the pitch and off it. He was always immaculately dressed. I'm not saying he didn't have a bit of a temper but that can be good in a footballer. It made him a fiery player and, when he learned to control it, this became a fantastic asset! As a footballer, well, he was not unlike Gary Lineker, except that he was heavier. He looked rather like an American football player in a way and had that special turn of pace to frighten high-quality defenders. His place had been in doubt in the promotion year but after his November burst of scoring it never was again.'

If Charlton, Bristol City and Scunthorpe could not catch the shooting star, the police could, for on December 6 Hitchens transgressed with a double-barrelled shotgun on land at Great Witley. He was summoned for taking game without licences and killing game on Sunday, dead-eye Hitchens having nabbed a hat-trick of pheasants the day after having an empty bag at Rotherham. He was fined £5 two months later but the incident provided an insight into the life of this softly-spoken man, who lived with his wife and first child in Hasbury, Halesowen.

It is also revealing that when asked by a reporter how he would spend £50, he said: 'If I had to spend it, I would buy the wife a new dress, get a baby-sitter and have a super night out. Theatre, the lot.' At this time, players were on a maximum wage of £20-a-week with a £4 win bonus. When Hitchens scored against his old club, Cardiff City, in a 2-0 win on December 12, 54,736 people were packed into Villa Park, such was the soaring interest in the man whose schoolboy experience of football was in the Boy Scouts. But it does make us wonder where all the receipts went.

Yes, there was always a touch of the Boy Scout about Hitchens. He was unfailingly polite, anxious to please, honourable, thrifty — and prepared. As ever, his team were fully prepared for the F.A. Cup as well. The first Saturday of the new decade started the fans humming with anticipation as McParland and Wylie goals accounted for Leeds United. Chelsea and Port Vale were dispatched on their own grounds before, on March 12, 69,732 attended the quarter-final match with Preston North End, won by Hitchens and McParland goals.

Gerry Hitchens in 1960.

This was, hindsight tells us, to be the decade of the last, glorious sunset of English football. There was no hooliganism, the national team were to be World Cup champions and money had not become the god of envy. In this benign atmosphere, the name of Hitchens was being gently lobbed as a possibility for the 1962 World Cup. A successful appearance in the Cup final would certainly have attracted further interest from the selectors whose fickleness was the equal of any Hollywood casting director's.

It was not to be. As in the year before, they lost 0-1, on this occasion to Wolves for whom Norman Deeley scored. Again, too, the conquerors of Villa went on to hoist the cup in front of the royal box at Wembley.

The disappointment did not run very deep, for Villa were back in the First Division on August 20, 1960, celebrating with a 3-2 home victory against Chelsea. If Villa found goals easy to come by in these early matches, they also found them easy to let in. Five went in at West Ham and five at Blackpool, replying twice in London and three times at the seaside before victories at home to West Ham and Everton redressed the balance. Whatever the feelings about the defence — and they had let in 31 goals in the ten games before September was out — Hitchens had practically set the cathedral bells in Colmore Row chiming with seven goals in the opening five games.

They may even have been heard in distant Italy, for British had become the fashion over there since the triumphs of John Charles with Juventus, and Villa's continental tour in the summer had alerted scouts in Europe to Hitchens' freebooting style.

His scoring consistency throughout the season and growing maturity in build-up play marked him now as a future international. He scored another hat-trick on October 22, three goals which were specially savoured by Villa fans because they came in the 6-2 humbling of Birmingham City. This victory, as it was followed immediately by the 2-0 defeat of Albion — Hitchens 1 — made late autumn a time of mellow fruitfulness.

Mercer had begun to reshape his team with the introduction of young professionals, and so the desolating run from Christmas to mid-March was not altogether surprising. Only a couple of Cup and League Cup victories brightened the winter but at least Hitchens kept scoring, two each against Wolves, Blackpool and Blackburn yielding a modest couple of points. In the end, Mercer had to be satisfied with ninth place, a tidy accomplishment which was polished by gaining the first League Cup.

Hitchens scored in every round but the two-legged final, but by this time he was no longer a Villa player. Through ten matches he had battled, only to miss the decisive affairs. These were held over until the start of the 1961-62 season, Villa losing 2-0 at Millmoor and requiring extra time for McParland to score the winner in front of 30,765 people at Villa Park. Such

Captain Johnny Haynes and Hitchens's England colleagues admire the Birmingham Mail Midland Footballer of the Year trophy won by Hitchens just before he left for Italian football.

was the public's general apathy to this new competition that it is doubtful whether many more cared.

The clamour for Hitchens to be picked for England was answered by his inclusion in the Football League team to meet the Scottish League. For the traditional match with Scotland, manager Walter Winterbottom decided to stand by Bobby Smith, the burly Spurs centre-forward was more renowned for his fearlessness than skill but, nevertheless, a potent force with the great Spurs team of the time.

On May 9, however, Hitchens was told by Winterbottom that he would play against Mexico the following day. Hitchens, normally so imperturbable, whooped with joy. Minutes later, he said: 'This is the day I have dreamed about for so long. It has been my life's ambition to play for England — and now I have the chance. I am deeply grateful to my Villa colleagues, the club and the fans for helping me to reach my target.'

He had, indeed, come a long way from Highley County School, Shropshire, where he could not get a game of football, a lad so honest that when West Bromich Albion tried to tempt him to sign he refused on the grounds that he had already promised Kidderminster.

By then Midland Footballer of the Year, outvoting such players as Don Howe and Bobby Robson, both of the Albion, and Ron Flowers, of Wolves, Hitchens, scorer of 42 goals that season, had induced in Villa-land a following of rock 'n roll star proportions. He scored in the first minute against Mexico in a team that included Robson, Bobby Charlton and Johnny Haynes and won 8-0. It was shortly after his debut international that he first heard of Italian interest in his signature.

Gerry said: 'I first heard from an Aston Villa official. Then they made a firm offer and it was up to me.' If the prospective purchasers, Internazionale Milan, were on tenterhooks when Hitchens scored twice in England's 3-2 victory in Italy, they became frantic. After one more England match, against Austria, the unassuming lad from a mining village decided to abandon the Halesowen garden in which he had so much pride, the shooting, golf, and his five-year-old 8 horsepower saloon car for Italy. In Milan, he would receive a £12,000 signing-on fee, a wage probably five times his Villa salary and football perspectives unobtainable in Britain, never mind Birmingham.

'I wanted to see different places and play against different teams,' said Hitchens, as Brum hearts bled. 'And I wanted the best possible standard of living for my wife and children.' Wife

Meriel and children Marcus and Nicola — Hitchens eventually had five children — soon joined him in an apartment in the exclusive Hotel Rosa. Having an English player in an Italian side was practically a status symbol that year, for Denis Law, Joe Baker and Jimmy Greaves also moved there from the island, none of them as successfully as Hitchens, who stayed for eight years with Inter Milan, Torino, Atlanta Bergamo and Cagliari and put down his acceptance there to the steadying influence of his family.

When they returned to England, Hitchens was 35 and after a short, part-time spell with Worcester City, he walked out of football as he had always said he would, and went back to his wife's home town of Pontypridd where he became a director of his father-in-law's fabrications firm and kept prize Afghan Hounds. I remember meeting him when Juventus came to Birmingham to play Villa in the home leg of their European Cup quarter-final in March, 1983. With him at a lunchtime function in their honour was John Charles, possibly the only British footballer to have a greater reputation in Italy.

'I never seriously regretted leaving Villa,' said Hitchens, a slim and extremely fit looking 48-year-old. 'I only regretted that I won no more than seven England caps and that the World Cup in Chile was such a disappointment.'

Unbelievably, Hitchens died a month later, on April 13, collapsing during a friendly football game for a solicitors' team.

He was mourned as a footballer who never made an enemy. How good was he? Eric Houghton thinks that only Pongo Waring was more dangerous as the wearer of a No. 9 shirt. 'Andy Gray wasn't as strong as Gerry,' he says. 'Hitchens was half a stone heavier but with his pace that was a big advantage. He had the sharpness that Peter Withe lacked and I don't think players like Derek Dougan and Tony Hateley were as good as any of them.'

Ron Wylie said: 'He always gave everything. He was quite brave and would burst his heart out for you, not in the way that

Gray was brave. Gray went where angels feared to tread. No, he was a non-stop trier who would be worth at least £2 million these days. He would definitely get into the current England team who would make a lot of use of his ability to run on to through balls and crack them in from 20 yards.'

Gerry Hitchens

Born Rawnsley, Staffs., 8th October 1934. Died April 1983. Bought from Cardiff City for £25,000. Debut 21st December 1957. League appearances 132, goals 78. F.A. Cup 18/7. F.L. Cup 10/11. Total 160/96. Seven England caps (3 with Villa). Second Division champions 1960. Sold to Inter Milan. (Also played for Torino, Atlanta, Cagliari. Midlands Player of Year 1961.

CHAPTER 5

Charlie Aitken

IN AUGUST, 1959, A 17-YEAR-OLD SCHOOL LAD caught the train from Edinburgh to Birmingham destined for a year's trial with Aston Villa. A rugby three-quarter from Watson's School in the Scottish capital, Charlie Aitken entertained only the faintest prospect of becoming a professional soccer player. Perhaps his pace and willingness, he hoped, would carry him through.

The early portents were not good. Charlie's background was of another planet to the boys around him, even when they could understand the accent, well-modified as it was. Aitken came from a family which must have been regarded as somewhat exotic even in the quadrangle of Watson's. His father had earned a satisfactory, if sometimes uncomfortable, living exporting Scottish champion bulls to South America. This involved journeying to Rio de Janeiro or Buenos Aires with the animals themselves, a task that inspires awe in visitors to Aitken's Moseley, Birmingham, home when he stands them before a photograph of one of the bulls whose hairy accoutrements are touching the ground, while Mr Aitken senior looks proudly on.

By the time Charlie, one of two sons, was taking the rather less arduous pioneer's journey to New Street station, his father had become manager of a cousin's farm. The excursion was to last longer than anyone could possible have imagined, for the curly-haired youngster would stay 17 years with Villa, amass a record 561 League appearances and still have a couple of years to play behind Pele with New York Cosmos when American soccer seemed an excitingly viable venture.

Even today Aitken does not really know why he continued to try to become a footballer; maybe it was a Scot's reaction to a challenge, maybe the stubborness that is also a quality of his race, maybe he found football the ideal outlet for his speed and stamina; probably a combination of the three. But with the offer of a return to Watson's, to rugby, grouse-beating, the combined cadet corps and 'highers' waiting for him, he chose to battle it out at Villa where no-one in authority seemed to take a blind bit of notice of him.

He admits he was not a natural footballer. Rugby had been more his game, the drawback being his parents' reaction to physical damage dished out to try to stop a young man with wings on his heels. A group of boys formed their own youth team and, after a year or so, Aitken was approached by Lothian United, one of Scotland's most successful junior sides and shortly to win the country's amateur cup for under-15s. No fewer than ten of the team were to turn professional, although Aitken at that stage seemed the likeliest to miss this graduation. He joined Hibernian's junior team, Edinburgh Thistle, regarding it as 'a bit of fun', and expected to continue his education from 'lowers' to 'highers' and probably university.

There was no call from Hibs, either, so that when Villa chief scout Jimmy Emson asked him to go to Villa, he was surprised. 'I was quick and fit and had a good left foot,' says Aitken today. 'My strongest assets were always my speed and recovery. I decided to try a year with Villa because I knew I could go back to school to finish my education.

'I came to Birmingham with Wilson Briggs who was much more talented than I was. He had a couple of games for Villa and then left. I think it was more difficult for me than for him, because I came from a totally different intellectual environment from most players. I had loved every second of

Charles the 1st. Jimmy Brown, Geoff Vowden and Chico Hamilton in the shirts that denoted Aitken's record-equalling appearances for Villa.

school and at Villa I was totally ignored in the first year. I was a fish out of water.'

Someone must have seen something of a swimmer in him, however, even in those days when the system of development was far more casual. Clubs could afford to run four or five teams — Aitken was duly and regularly selected for the fifths — and youths were wasted into the outside world, as if they were so many bananas. Survival was as much a matter of self-discipline and determination as football ability but young players also required character that was resilient enough to stand rough treatment.

'Perhaps I saw a glimmer of hope, I don't know,' says Aitken, 'but it was touch and go whether I stayed or not. Then we went on a youth tour of Holland and I played quite well at centre-half. In fact, I learned later that Newcastle offered money for me and I was still only in the third team. I felt I was improving and the staff, Joe Mercer who was manager, Dick Taylor and Ray Shaw, put in a lot of work on me. I spent hours striking the ball with my left foot although little else. It was a basic type of game then.

'Eventually Joe decided to give me a game in the first team, against Sheffield Wednesday on the last day of the 1960-61 season. We won 4-1, Gerry Hitchens playing for the last time for Villa. He couldn't stop scoring that season. He was strong and quick but I was so fast I used to laugh at the first team. I once ran past Bobby Thomson and nicked the ball off him. He still tells me now he wanted to kick me up the backside.'

For Villa fans the match was doubly historic. Hitchens left for Italy and the big paydays, Johnny Dixon for the comparable anonymity of coaching young players at Villa. Dixon had been with his only league club for 17 years, and how fitting it was that he should unwittingly be passing on the Lions baton — collected from Frank Broome. Aitken who would himself link up with Gordon Cowans in the same way, four players exactly covering 56 years of first-team football, bar the spell Cowans spent with Bari in Italy.

'I know from the record that Johnny scored a goal on that day against Wednesday. We realised Joe was getting rid of him. They say youth is wasted on the young and the fact is that I didn't understand the significance of the occasion. Johnny lived and died football,' says Aitken.

Mercer decided the time had come to revitalise a club that seemed happy to be respectable. Aitken was among a host of inexperienced young players the manager brought in to provide running power. Out went Dixon, Stan Lynn, Peter McParland and John Neal: in came Aitken, John Sleeuwenhoek, Alan Baker and Harry Burrows. Reporters searching for alliteration called them 'Mercer's Minors' and 'Mercer's Marvels' but if it were a second edition of the Busby Babes they were looking for, Villa proved an illusion.

Aitken made his second appearance in a 4-3 League Cup victory against Bradford City on September 13, beginning a sequence that was to remain relatively undisturbed until January 31st, 1976, when Ron Saunders decided peremptorily that the best playing servant in Villa history was surplus to

Villa fans took Aitken to their hearts. Here, he holds aloft the 1962 Terrace Trophy.

requirements and picked him for just one reserve match for the rest of the season. Aitken remains bitter about the experience.

That is to race ahead of the story. The Villa of Saunders' time might just have been in a different millennium to Mercer's. The terraces were friendly places to inhabit in 1961, no filthy songs, no fighting drunks, no collective violence. Fans of both sides mingled at the Holte End and the policemen, having rested against the perimeter wall of the pitch, appeared only to patrol the touchlines five minutes before half-time and the final whistle.

The game itself had not seriously advanced technically from the W-formation of the founders, despite the laceration to national pride inflicted by the two Hungarian thrashing of England six years earlier. Tom Finney at Preston had employed the deep central role of Hideguti with success at Preston but British discomfort at change is emphasised by the name they gave to Finney's new position — deep-lying centre-forward. How a 'deep-lying' player could be central and forward was a mystery I never unfolded.

Mercer was among those managers, moulded by pre-war football, who were initially thrown off balance by the sudden wave of change that overtook our football, accelerated by Alf Ramsey's decision to do away with wing-play in favour of mobility. Ramsey, we now know, took English club football down a blind alley, for slavish adherence to the method he used to counterbalance the lack of wingers led to the sterility of the high ball down the middle.

At the start of the 1961 season, though, Mercer had three years ahead at Villa Park. The classical wing-half of Everton and Arsenal still loved to impress his players with the skills that once hushed Highbury. 'There was nothing Joe liked better than training in the car park,' says Aitken. 'On Friday morning we weren't allowed to leave until his side had won. Joe was all right. He kept picking me every week, didn't he?

'After one bad match, he said to me: "Do you know, Charlie, they should chop off your right leg and use it as firewood?" On the Monday, he apologised to me. But there was some truth in what he said. I was a great one for playing within my ability.

'It was a totally different world in those days. Kids of 12-14 know more today than I did when I was 20. We played because we liked the game, whereas so many of lads are money-orientated today. I found the uncertainty of football a problem, though. Insecurity was always present because of our

The lad made friends easily.

contract terms. They were a joke, they were so much in favour
of the clubs. We could play in front of 60,000 people and pick
up £10 after tax and, if we won, a £4 bonus. It wasn't until
Jimmy Hill threatened to lead a strike that we won the
unlimited wage in 1962. I was the players' union representative
and I know that trying to get a fair deal was like trying to get
blood out of a stone.

'Clubs abused the money they received and Villa were one
of the worst. The board was an embarrassment. They didn't
have a clue in my opinion. They were perfectly happy to plod
along as a middle-of-the-table club, never really bent on
success. At about that time they sold the Hercules training
ground for houses without any replacement. Where we had a
couple of training pitches of our own close by, from then on we
had to borrow pitches from firms such as Dunlop or Delta
Metals. It was a nightmare.

'Johnny Haynes became the first £100-a-week footballer,

and what a fuss there was about that. We received £3-50 basic. We were sick and tired of being abused and most of us would genuinely have gone on strike. For instance, contracts were for a year with a year's option for the club. They held the player's registration papers which meant they could stop you playing again for life. Then the fund handed out £750 at 35.'

The 1962 team included a number of men due to become highly influential in the development of the game. Dougan was a reforming chairman of the players' union while Welsh international Phil Woosnam moved to the US where he was Commissioner of the North American Soccer League and manager of the US national side. Vic Crowe was for a while Woosnam's assistant at the NASL, later becoming Villa manager, and right-back Gordon Lee, John Neal and Ron Wylie were also to hold positions as managers of First Divison teams.

Dougan was best known at Villa Park for appearing with a totally shaven head but the re-growth did not, according to Aitken, inspire greater commonsense. 'Derek was an enigma,' he says. 'He could have been world class had he applied himself on the pitch rather than other things. I don't relate to that side of the game. He couldn't or wouldn't play against certain centre-halves, either. He would always have a bad back on the day before he was to face Charlie Hurley of Sunderland.'

Alf Ramsey's Ipswich were League champions that season, but while Spurs continued to dominate domestic football, Wolves and Burnley were in the Indian Summer of fame, both to decline gradually, while Liverpool, Everton and Leeds took up the challenge of great sides produced at Old Trafford and White Hart Lane.

Aitken was quick to pick up the disciplines of defending. He liked to 'nick' the ball from forwards, his speed and intelligence providing the opportunity to steal the ball and recover, rather than electing for outright confrontation and loss of control of the ball. A by-product of this technique was that it gave referees unhindered view of the tackle and, subsequently, rare reason to award free-kicks or penalties.

Aitken did, however, give away one bizarre penalty, although it proved to be inexpensive for it was in an end-of-season match that brought an 8-3 win for Villa against Leicester City in 1962. The home side were three ahead when young Aitken slid on his backside on wet turf, intending to push up the ball after it had passed over the goal-line. He mistimed his grab and to his horror handled the ball six inches inside his own area.

Usually, he was a skinflint in his own half. He had, true Scotsman, a ready eye for percentages. 'I never hacked anyone down in my own area,' he says. 'The odds were always better on letting a chap go through to try to beat the 'keeper. I remember that later I tried to teach John Gidman, a very skilful player, not to hold on to the ball in his own area. There's a right time to knock the ball out of play.'

The Sixties, the decade of the Beatles, Carnaby Street, the World Cup, and, allegedly, peace, love and friendship, was probably the worst decade in the illustrious history of Villa. It opened brightly enough with promotion back to Division One, but ended as Villa were about to drop into Divison Three for the first time. Aitken and Alan Deakin were the only two players to bridge this era of failure that began with Joe Mercer and saw the departure of Mercer, Dick Taylor, Tommy Cummings and Tommy Docherty before Vic Crowe took over and revived fortunes with the introduction of three or four wonderfully talented young players.

There was an inner darkness to football in the early Sixties, too. This was never better exemplified than by a Villa experience at Hillsborough when a centre-forward cheerfully known as 'Bronco' Layne smashed his fist into Jimmy MacEwan's face, apparently because he didn't like it. MacEwan, a lean, angular Scottish winger, reached up to his mouth to discover four broken teeth. Neither referee nor linemen had spotted the incident and they must have been as puzzled as the rest of the crowd when MacEwan erupted in rage and began to chase Lane. The referee caught up with him first and, examining the Sheffield Wednesday player's knuckles, discovered deep teeth marks and sent him off.

The crowd reacted with a 13-minute riot that Aitken describes as his most frightening experience on a football field. Cushions rained down from the stand newly-built for the World Cup. It was MacEwan's last match for Villa and very nearly Lane's for Wednesday. Soon afterwards, the bulky centre-forward was found guilty of accepting bribes to lose a football match and, along with two others, sent to jail.

But Aitken believes there were other cases of this sort: 'It was rife in the lower divisions of England and also in Scotland. I know players who have been offered £100s at half-time to throw games. I don't want to say more than that.'

When Mercer, suffering from a nervous breakdown, left Villa in 1964, the team had finished 19th. 'He took it very personally,' says Aitken. 'He was a real gentleman and later was highly successful with Manchester City and England, probably one of the best England managers there has been, because he picked the most skilful players. But by then at Villa he would pass you in the corridor and not recognise you.

'Dick Taylor took over. He was in much the same mould but lacked ruthlessness. It was a cut-throat business. After him came Tommy Cummings and we went badly into a slide. Cummings was a drinker and the players had little respect for him.

'As for Tommy Docherty, well for the first time there was excitement around, the feeling that something was happening. We started to react on the pitch and he and Arthur Cox knew how to organise a defence. Docherty wasn't a great manager at Villa, though. That much is obvious, because we went down to the Third the season he was sacked. Nevertheless, he was a character and a great motivator.

'My attitude always was that I would play as well as I could for any manager. It was my job and I left as soon after work as I could. I didn't hang about. I had other interests outside football. It wasn't the be-all and end-all of my life.

New manager — Ron Saunders — and a change of strip . . . Frank Carrodus makes up a cheerful threesome. Later, relationships deteriorated.

There are more interesting things than talking about football all the time and I just got bored to tears with the subject.

'Cummings once said to me in the changing room: "What sport do you really like, Charlie?" and I replied: "Rugby". There was a great cheer from the other lads but it was true. I was brought up on it and I still go and watch it.'

Tony Hateley was Villa's only high scorer of this period. No-one but he, a remarkable header of the ball, managed even twenty goals in a season. Hateley hopped about football clubs almost as much as around the penalty area, but there was no denying his use as a sort of low-flying missile launcher. Tall and clumsy on the ground, he was a skylark off it and for two years Villa maximised his use and held on to their First Division place.

Aitken regards him as one of the greatest headers he ever saw. 'In training he could jump so that two-feet of him showed over the bar,' says Aitken. 'We knew how to use him, too. He was the only man I ever saw score with a header from outside the box. The ball was crossed and, wallop, it was in the net.'

Hateley scored four goals in a match that still prompts sighs for long-departed dramas from those who took part. Goals from Tottenham's Alan Gilzean, Jimmy Greaves, Frank Saul, Laurie Brown and Jimmy Robertson had received but a single response, from Hateley, before much second-half action was under way. Then Deakin and Hateley made it 5-3, and Hateley's head directed two more to turn a White Hart Lane jamboree into a heart-stopper.

Aitken takes up the story: 'It sounds amazing but I was standing by Jimmy Greaves at the near post for a corner soon after their fifth goal. Greaves said: "You still have a chance. The centre of our defence isn't playing at all well." Actually we went very close to victory, because Alan Deakin ran around their goalkeeper, Pat Jennings, in the dying seconds and rolled it towards goal before Cyril Knowles just managed to kick it off the line.'

Six weeks later, in the penultimate match of the 1965-66 season, Manchester United followed the 7-0 trouncing of the year before with a 6-1 victory at Old Trafford. This was the United of Best and Charlton, a team destined to win the championship the following year.

'They used to annihilate us,' says Aitken. 'Best had this terrific ability to stop and change direction. He would go past your weighted foot and he was so fit and strong in those days, you couldn't just knock him off the ball. He's the only player I met who would deliberately play a one-two off your legs. He had superb balance, just like Pele. Pele actually made the hair on my neck stand on end. He was 35 when I was in his team at New York Cosmos and he scored with a double scissors. The ball was going past him when he stopped it, turned and performed this double-scissors in mid-air. Breathtaking.'

No such gymnastics were required of less gifted men in 1966-67, for teams of decidedly utilitarian mode, Chelsea, Stoke and Southampton, to name three, were capable of smacking half-a-dozen past Villa's bewildered side, from whom Taylor had allowed Chelsea to extract Hateley for £100,000. Even Aitken was used in attack in an effort to cajole the 'goals for' total into taking over. These were grim days and becoming grimmer. Villa lost seven of their last nine games, a time during which, Aitken claims, certain financial promises were made but not fulfilled.

The appointment of Cummings brought no relief. While English football basked in the afterglow of World Cup success, Villa sought a redeemer and found, instead, a false prophet. Cummings was sacked in November 1968 and, with coach Arthur Cox in temporary charge, a public meeting of Villa fans at Digbeth Civic Hall demanded change. They got it, in the form of a huge public shares issue, Doug Ellis, as chairman for the first of three times, and Pat Matthews, with ex-player Harry Parkes, as two of the directors. They promptly appointed Tommy Docherty to take over, after only a month at QPR after leaving Chelsea.

The larger-than-life Docherty was initially successful. A run of victories took Villa out of immediate trouble and, employing such revolutionary tactics as man-for-man marking, he and Cox locked the defence so tightly that in their final 10 matches they let in only seven. The trouble was that they scored only six, and a peculiar kind of history was made when Villa's leading League marksman — if he may be called that — beat the opposition keepers only five times. Ten years earlier Gerry Hitchens had done that in one match. Birmingham fans clearly enjoyed self-flagellation because 52,772 of them rolled up for the Villa-Blues local derby match.

Even The Doc must have been lost for words by the start to that fateful 1969-70 season. His team scored four goals in the opening eight League matches — that made it ten goals in 1,710 minutes of Second Division football — and there was little improvement afterwards. Docherty made his jokes about Ellis's advice 'I am right behind you, Tommy.' The reply remains one of Docherty's party pieces: 'I want you in front of me where I can see you.' But by January, with only 18 points taken out of 54, the inevitability of his departure was confirmed.

There was not sufficient time for his successor, former captain Vic Crowe, to interrupt the decline and Villa left the Second Division with Preston North End, a team of equal nineteenth-century eminence who, like Villa, were Double winners.

'It was my worst time in football,' says Aitken. 'I thought "my God, how terrible. The Third Divison." We had never been able to win often enough away from home. That was true right up to the time Ron Saunders became manager. There wasn't the mental attitude or concentration. We should have come straight back up, but didn't. We were skilful enough but lacked the right application.'

Yet if ever a club needed a real shock, it was Aston Villa. Unused to the muddy outposts of soccer, to Barnsley, Halifax, Wrexham and Torquay, they never quite got their bearings, although Crowe's sensible buying and sound coaching gradually restored the inner strength of the club. Andy Lochhead and Chico Hamilton began to look like a threatening partnership and a steady defence ensured fourth place. Even in the bad times, however, traditionally big clubs always seem to find a way of providing a reminder that they are not dead, merely slumbering.

Villa's proof was a League Cup run that included a two-leg aggregate victory over Manchester United in the semi-final. Aitken remembers the 1-1 draw at Manchester United as one of the great performance of his years at the club, while the 2-1 victory at Villa Park on December 23 was a premature celebration of Christmas. Brian Kidd put United ahead in the first half but Lochhead and McMahon, with a powerful 73rd-minute header, ensured Villa's first visit to Wembley in 14 years.

In the final, Spurs defeated Villa 2-0, yet Aitken contends he enjoyed this final much more than the visit four years later when his side beat Norwich 1-0.

Aitken ready for action in 1974.

His record in the League Cup is spectacular, for he has played no fewer than 61 times, scoring one goal, at Hartlepool, in the year Villa won the trophy. 'I came from a deep position and beat the keeper with my right foot,' he remembers, mildly emphasising 'right foot' — the one Mercer advocated should be firewood.

Villa were on the rise. Next season Aitken scored four goals, having struck up a good understanding with left-winger Willie Anderson, who scored 16 himself. Crowe blended youth and experience expertly, offending many fans by swapping skipper Brian Godfrey for Ray Graydon, a move that was made after the manager had checked with Aitken for his opinion. Graydon and Anderson formed the rare double act, scoring wingers, while Lochhead, Hamilton and Geoff Vowden contributed plenty of goals as well. Nine wins in their final 11 matches allowed Villa to romp back to the Second Division with a record number of points.

They also set a Third Division crowd record with 48,110 against Bournemouth, averaging 31,952 for the season. Aitken says: 'I remember the Bournemouth match for another reason. Vic Crowe asked me to man-mark Phil Boyer who, with Ted McDougall, made a lethal partnership. Boyer was incredible. He received 90 per cent of the throw-ins and worked like no man I have seen. He must have covered every blade of grass. I destroyed his effectiveness but it is the first time I ever had to concentrate on stopping someone playing for the entire 90 minutes. I preferred to be more creative.

'The crowds were tremendous and the city buzzed for us but it was never true that the fans would turn up to watch 11 claret and blue shirts on the line. Nothing like true. That year was just very special.'

Villa were within a place of promotion again the following season, although this state was a little flattering because they finished 11 points behind QPR, who were second in Division Two. Aitken remembers it particularly because he acquired a knee ligament injury, the cause of one of the rare occasions on which he missed more than a couple of matches. 'Some players create their own injuries by stupidity,' he says. 'They take up suicidal positions and are very susceptible. I am a great admirer of Bryan Robson but sometimes his confrontations are not to his own good. People can get carried away with their own temper. I preferred to steal the ball.'

The next season was less successful. Crowe had assembled a side of formidable potential and, indeed, with the introduction of Little and Gidman, destined both to be England players albeit for only a match, there appeared to be the basis of a challenge for promotion again. It was not to be. Villa finished below halfway, yet Saunders was to reap the

Left foot in control.

benefit of Crowe's judgement. How often do we hear sacked managers say they have left the club stronger than when they joined it. In Crowe's case this was manifestly true. The trouble was Ellis and Birmingham felt they could not wait.

Aitken, who missed only four games that season, shares the opinion that Crowe was unfortunate to be dismissed but declines to criticise Ellis. 'He has his critics but he has always worked for Villa morning, noon and night. He has stuck at it and in the end he got the better of Ron Saunders. His heart is in the right place.'

So Crowe left the club he had skippered and managed with some distinction and in his place Ellis and the board appointed Ron Saunders. It was, in its way, like the Coal Board appointing Arthur Scargill. Initially, there was sweetness and light, later a succession of explosive incidents which reshaped the old club but also pervaded it with a feeling of inner conflict.

Aitken was not to know it, but 1974-75 would be his spectacular sunset at Villa Park, although he was a lingering presence for another year. The confidence and apparent certainty of success that Saunders brought with him from a short career of spiteful infighting at Maine Road were remarkable. Graydon found it hard to miss goal in the first half of the season, Little in the second. Villa were promoted behind Tommy Docherty's fearless young Manchester United side, finishing the League season by winning 12 of their 14 fixtures and bringing home the League Cup from Wembley into the bargain.

But the return season in the First Division proved to be a trial. 'In the first year Ron had been amicable and friendly,' says Aitken. 'He did a good job and there was rapport. He was very organised and got the best out of players such as Keith Leonard whom he worked very hard. Personally, I played football for satisfaction and enjoyment.

'Then things went very wrong. I think he hated me because I was more popular than him. The same was true of Giddy. I knew I had finished at Villa when he called me into his office in December and said "I have decided you can stay here as long as you want." The writing was on the wall.'

If ever Aitken wondered about his interpretation of this coded warning, he was soon to find out when Saunders took hold of an enemy's throat he did not let go.

'At 33, I was still the fittest man on his books,' he says. 'Saunders waited until one hour before the transfer deadline before telling me he was giving me a free transfer. What chance had I of finding another club? I didn't get another game. He's a ruthless man. He once made one of his assistants act as a goalpost for 90 minutes because he had dared to answer him back.'

So Aitken's 17 years ended in solitary goodbyes and some deathbed humour from the lads he had watched grow into a team. Not that he was ever a man to sit and recriminate. Within weeks, he had joined New York Cosmos where Pele was still shining as the greatest player of all. For two wonderful years Aitken chased the ball across artificial turf in, it must be admitted, an artifical setting. The surface troubled his knees and the heat prickled his sensitive Celtic skin, but he was a footballer reborn.

Charlie Aitken

Born Edinburgh 1st May 1942. Debut 29th April 1961. League appearances 559 + 2 sub, goals 14. F.A. Cup 34 + 1/1. FL Cup 61/1. Europe 2/0. Total 656 + 3/16. 3 Scottish under-23 caps. Record Villa appearances, League Cup tankard 1975, Third Division champions 1972, Second Division promotion 1975. Villa Terrace Trophy winner 1962. Midlands Player of Year 1975. Joined New York Cosmos 1976.

CHAPTER 6

Brian Little

WHEN THE CLARET-AND-BLUE MANAGER IN the sky names the club's greatest eleven, he will risk the unbridled wrath of those of us who followed Villa in the Seventies if Brian Little is omitted from his list. His playing career harrowingly cut short at 27, Little still registers the highest marks for ball-control, style and an unconquerable belief that football was the thing.

Where fans held Gray in awe, Chris Nicholl in admiration and Dennis Mortimer in respect, Little was loved by every kid, old and young, who recognised how sweet it was to slide away from a tackle or deliver a perfectly-placed pass. I can see Little in my mind's eye, blue-jowled, socks tight to just below the knee, shirt hanging to his thighs, coasting to the by-line to roll pinpoint passes to Gray or Deehan or Graydon. He scored lots of goals, too, but those were never the sole objective of his game. He enjoyed creating the tapestry as much as completing it.

Little was also an enigma or, as he puts it: 'An awkward little so-and-so. I still am to an extent. I suppose I don't always do what people expect of me: the opposite sometimes.'

On a football field, this may be as infuriating to the manager as it is to the opposition. Unpredictability was by no means Little's only weapon but how he liked to tease with the sudden move outside his marker, or to touch the ball behind his

Early in the first team life of Brian.

own leading leg and throw his opponents off-balance, sometimes to the confusion of his own team-mates as well. Today, there is hardly a player like him; perhaps Peter Beardsley is nearest in his ability to be devastating in the open spaces few others can find.

Little's first-team career at Villa Park spanned the top of Division Three — he played one full match in 1971-72 — to the top of Division One, although a serious knee injury prevented his appearance in a single game nine years later, before he finally was forced to retire. He scored 82 goals in a career of 301 matches but, in reality, he was completely free from injury for only four seasons in which he played 192 games and scored 69 times. In two of those seasons, Villa won the League Cup, and while he contributed strongly towards the success in 1974-75, no-one at the club, I fancy, would deny that 1976-77 was the Little Spectacular.

Not only did he score ten goals, missing out in only one round, he also accepted the spearhead role in the second replay of the final, scoring twice in a famously thrilling 3-2 win against Everton.

'That was a classic match,' he says. 'The Everton full back Neil Robinson works with me at Darlington and I often remind him that he gave me the ball for my first. Another of my staff, Jim Willis, was an Everton ball boy at Old Trafford and I regularly see Terry Darracott the left back. It's a standing joke between us because he left the ball for me to put in just before the end of extra time. "Leave that one Terry," I say. He laughs now but I don't think he did at the time.

'I don't remember a thing about the Cup Final at Wembley. It was a dreadful occasion. The replay at Hillsborough wasn't a lot better.

'In the first round we came up against Manchester City who had given us a right beating at Maine Road in the League. I had so little to do I was practically a passenger, so I had time to watch Dennis Tueart on City's wing. He was brilliant that day and I tried hard to copy him in the next match, the way

Going for goal, left-footed.

he moved to the left and suddenly swept to his right in two strides.

'It worked as well because I had a good game against them in the League Cup. We won 3-0.'

Manager Ron Saunders said that night at Villa Park: 'Brian still has a lot to learn. He did well, like so many of my players, but in a couple of years' time he could be something really special. He's 100 per cent fit again now and it's a question of him increasing his experience at First Division level.'

Saunders was ever a man for commending with faint praise but even he must have acknowledged the quality of those two goals. In the 33rd minute, Graydon swung over a right-wing corner, Nicholl headed to the far post and there was Little, facing away from goal, to roll over backwards and hook the ball over his left shoulder into the top corner of Joe Corrigan's goal. If the huge goalkeeper was taken aback with that one, imagine his feelings when 13 minutes later Little back to his goal again, flicked Nicholl's long pass with the back of his heel, leaving defender Mike Doyle floundering, before measuring his low drive wide of Corrigan.

Afterwards in the press room, experienced reporters were whispering the name 'George Best' in the same breath as Little's and although this comparison has been made numerous times with players without an ounce of Best's unique skills, in Little's case the similarities were as notable as the differences. Best was more of a competitor than the self-effacing Little; he had an extra few inches of speed and proved himself consistently against the greatest players. Yet Little was as balanced, as beguilingly Rolls Royce in his movements and created and killed with the same voracity. If not quite the genuine article, he was an immensely gifted reproduction. Four years later, Little's career was in ruins, as prematurely as Best's was, but not of his own violition.

Meanwhile, past Norwich, Wrexham and Millwall, Villa cruised with nine goals for and only two against — Little three of them, Gray three, as well — until February 1 when they began a series of three semi-final ties against the then-formidable Queens Park Rangers. 'We always seemed to be ahead only to be pegged back,' says Little who finally stopped the show with a hat-trick at Highbury on February 22.

'It's an odd thing, when we had something to celebrate I often sat in front of the bus by myself. I don't really know whether I did it on purpose, it was probably doing the opposite of what was expected. But I also liked to review things in my own time, particularly if we'd won. It's all right celebrating but sometimes it's better to remember everything that happened rather than just wake up with a headache.'

Little's football was rather like that. For all that he formed a devastating partnership with Gray, he was always a man you felt could do things alone, only a slow smile to mark the latest accomplishment.

Little established himself as a Villa first-team player the year before the club's second-ever League Cup success, in

Typical Little turn between opponents.

1974-75. His brother, Alan, made three appearances in that run, too, scoring his only goal for the club from the No. 9 position before disappearing to the lower divisions.

Saunders was well aware of what a potentially good player he had inherited before the rest of England outside Birmingham realised in the dying days of the season that the city possessed not one, Trevor Francis, but two of the country's outstanding young forwards. Little scored 10 goals in a six-match spell as Villa swept from the Second Division on a tide of eight consecutive wins to follow that League Cup success.

Little says: 'I started the season badly. I was injured against Orient and I couldn't get my place back. Then it was my 21st birthday on November 25 when we won 6-1 at home to Hartlepool in the third round. Our kid played his second game in that match. Ray Graydon, Chico Hamilton and I scored a couple apiece.

'Our kid got one in the quarter final against Colchester

and then we had a couple of semi-final battles against Chester. As I remember it, we were two-up in the second leg at Villa Park and I stabbed in the winner.

'Overall, we had a good side. Keith Leonard took a lot of the weight off me. He was a good leader of the line, always prepared to take a bit of punishment, like big Peter Withe was. Ray Graydon scored a lot of goals that year, including the one that won the final. He was great at picking up little goals. He must have stuck in no-end by running to his post on to crosses from the other side. He was exceptional with it. Then there was Giddy, who loved to have fun on the right, dashing across the pitch.'

But the meteor was Brian Little, no question about that. To his credit, England manager Don Revie recognised it and didn't dally. He called Little into his full squad, along with Francis and Gidman, for the Home International championships.

Little had a problem, for when he proposed to Heather Watson, the possibility that their wedding might clash with England international selection had not entered his head. So they brought the day forward and by the time Little played his one and only game for his country, he was a married man.

That one appearance was noteworthy for its impact and its brevity. If in 19 minutes a young man can look to the manner born, then Little was a young prince. David Johnson headed in his curling cross for the equaliser against Wales in the 86th minute and it was not only the Birmingham papers who predicted an illustrious career for the dark-haired intense-looking son of Durham.

At the time, he said: 'I was very surprised to play. I was sitting next to big Mal (Malcolm Macdonald) and I expected him to get on. I didn't feel at all nervous. It was great.'

He had won an unofficial race with Francis to wear the England shirt. 'I must admit I expected Trevor to be first,' added Little. 'I didn't expect to be with the England squad at all. I thought I would be on my honeymoon.'

Alex Stepney wins a challenge.

It seems incredible today that he was never again to appear for England in any guise. 'I didn't get another shout,' he says. 'I was selected for an under-23 match soon afterwards but I injured my knee against Everton and that was it.

'I still say I was never nervous before a match. I was always comfortable with the ball at my feet, never frightened of it. I was taught to master a football, always to be in control.

'It doesn't seem to matter today, though, does it? I've a centre-back at Darlington, a tough, willing lad but not very good with the ball at his feet. He's mobile, tall and a good header of the ball and that seems to be enough in today's football. I've turned down a lot of offers for him. Just to think, I've seen Sid Cowans control the ball in the air with a pot on his foot.

'Football has become a power sport in which you can actually win games by physical presence. Still, as soon as they join me I go to work on techniques. In fact, I only work on techniques — knocking the ball to feet and making them control it. They work so hard on Saturdays, some of them, that it takes days to get over it. Still, that's the easy side, fitness.

'In the days I was picked for England there were players who had the freedom to roam. I remember Eric Gates at Ipswich playing behind the front two, all over the pitch.'

Nineteen minutes. In the time it takes to smoke two cigarettes, Little had begun and ended his England career. There was an outcry to put him in against Scotland on the Saturday, three days after the Welsh match, but manager Don Revie hardly gave his selection a second thought.

Revie dismissed speculation with these comments: 'Little did exceptionally well against Wales. In my opinion, the lad got a taste on Wednesday and that is just enough for the moment. The atmosphere will be different tomorrow.'

Perhaps it seems hard to forgive Revie for his condescension, yet England won 5-1 at Hampden Park and the manager could ignore his critics. Little returned to Heather, formerly a Villa Park secretary, and his honeymoon. Next season, many of us thought, would be the beginning of a new England partnership: Francis and Little.

But 90 minutes, never mind a week or a season, is a long time in football. The Francis partnership was never forged and, worse, the one between Little and Leonard was lost when Leonard's knee was irreparably damaged. As if fate hadn't tortured Villa sufficiently, within three matches of Gray joining the club, Little himself suffered the first of those knee injuries which were eventually to twist his face in pain after every game.

By the time he returned, Villa were out of the Cup and League Cup and placed dangerously close to the foot of the First Division. Eight draws and three wins in the last 13 games were sufficient to retain their place but, again, in the 2-3 defeat by Birmingham City, Little was injured. Yet Gray and Little had seen enough of each other to convince them that they could work some magic together. And how!

Little says of the Scot, his opposite in almost every conceivable way both on and off the field: 'Andy was the easiest striker of them all. You just had to spot where he was and put the ball in front of him. For a passer, the margin of error was tremendous, like no-one else I have ever played alongside. You could give him the ball at anything from nought to ten yards and it was his. I enjoyed being a creator more than a scorer but don't get me wrong, I loved to knock them in.'

'But where Andy was an extrovert, I wasn't. I admit I'm not the sort to enliven a party. I just sit in a corner and chat. I suppose I express myself on a football field where I'm as arrogant as anyone.'

Gray's view of the wraith-like Little is equally complimentary: 'He was my first partner in English football and he did more than anyone to establish my reputation as a goalscorer. You could never meet a more unselfish player. If Brian was clear through and I was there with him, he wouldn't attempt to do anything too difficult to score himself. He would just slip the ball to me to do the job. He was never rewarded with the international acclaim he deserved. He won just one cap as a substitute which is ridiculous when you think that had he played for Liverpool, Manchester United or Spurs he could have been at least as effective as Kevin Keegan and had some of his recognition. He really could do incredible things with a football. I often wondered whether he had the ambition to go anywhere in football but I think he's proving me wrong.'

Little has a modest nature but knows the true worth of a player of his own potency, so he remains mildly surprised that in 1976-77 there was not further international recognition, especially as Don Revie would have been due to take England to the World Cup except that there were one or two snags on the way.

Despite the vast array of changes made by the England manager in a failed campaign to qualify for the European championship, Little was never one of them. Neither, after Revie absconded in the middle of the World Cup qualifying round did his successor, Ron Greenwood, call on the Geordie. Which reinforces Gray's comment about playing for favoured clubs.

Gray was undoutedly the star turn of that season, the Sundance Kid to Little's Butch Cassidy. There were few raindrops on anyone's head, either, for Dennis Mortimer was now integrated into the side, playing only one match fewer than the ever-present Little. And while Villa's untidy defence — they let in 50 goals and won only five matches away from home — cost them the championship, secured, of course, by Liverpool, they were by a fair distance the highest scorers in the division.

The bloom stayed on Villa no longer than the following summer, for the team who looked destined for greatness faded unaccountably, a poor start emphasising Saunders' determination to refashion his side. Typically Little, always the big-match player, saved his best for the UEFA Cup, scoring goals in the aggregate 6-0 defeat of Fenerbahce, and performing with his usual fluency against Gornik Zabrze and Atletico Bilbao before Barcelona came to Villa Park, Johan Cruyff and all, earning a 2-2 draw in a fourth-round first-leg tie that had nearly 50,000 people agog with excitement.

Behind the scenes, however, the club was in turmoil. The manager was engaged in a trial of wills with Gray and Gidman. It was Saunders' way to turn to Scotland or his native Liverpool when he needed players — Londoners were

High-flying Little with a header of Gray proportions.

practically *persona non grata* — and so, as Gidman of Liverpool and Gray of Glasgow were making preparation for the exits, perhaps unknown to them, so Allan Evans, of Dunfermline, and Des Bremner, of Banffshire, were making their entrances. Bremner was to become the essential midfield runner, McNaught and Evans an all-Scottish central defence on which the championship of '80-81 was founded.

Little, never booked in a first-team match, had a placid temperament which hid a stubborn streak as wide as the Tyne. He watched the comings and goings with tolerance as seething politics took over at Villa Park. He was never a member of a pro-Saunders clique, for clearly he had reservations which even today he does not see fit to publish. 'Ron Saunders overall was okay,' he says. 'Once you've had a job like his, things look different. At times I could be an awkward so-and-so. I don't think I ever misbehaved particularly. I wasn't bad but I was, and I still can be, headstrong. I always stuck to my story and sometimes that's a little hard for a manager to take.

'In the manager's job you have to be alert and ruthless. He was. I must say, though, he looked after me and certainly helped enormously when I had to stop playing. I don't shout about him and I certainly won't in future.'

Gray did not appear against Barcelona at Villa Park or Nou Camp and that, essentially, marked the end of the Gray-Little partnership, dramatic, glorious and brief. They played together 24 more times, but in '77-78 they scored a combined total of 29 goals — Little 11 — and the next season only 11 altogether. Both of them were in trouble with their knees, too. Little was out for two lengthy spells, at the end of 1978 and for more than a month at the end of the season.

Saunders was offloading player after player at this time. One of them, he decided, was to be Brian Little whose style had caused Birmingham City manager Jim Smith to dream of the perfect replacement for Trevor Francis, by then sold to Brian Clough at Forest for a few pounds short of £1 million. Smith was a sucker for skill and Little, still only 25, would have been a capture to compare with Frank Worthington, Colin Todd and Archie Gemill whom he also took to St Andrew's. The difference was that they were men coming to the end of their best years; Little was, or should have been, in his.

I well remember the fuss this projected £600,000 transfer caused in the city. Little was beloved of Villa fans as few have been. As Smith perceived, he had style, a quality St Andrew's, stuck above the terraced houses and industrial decay of inner-Brum, conspicuously lacked. Frankly, it was felt there could only be two reasons why Saunders would let Little go: either the knee, or what the manager regarded as disloyalty, perhaps both.

Certainly, the fact that Gray had overcome a fitness test and had signed for Wolves would have encouraged Saunders to believe that most things were possible when a chasing manager became obsessed by a goalscorer's talents. And Jim Smith would be just as persuasive with his chairman, the likeable Keith Coombs, as ever John Barnwell could be with Harry

Little in first again.

Marshall, chairman at Molineux. As for disloyalty, Little had opinions which he would express to the manager but he was a loner, not a plotter.

So in Birmingham, we prepared for a story which might have been headlined 'To knee or not to knee'. What happened next left us, Smith, Little and Saunders in various states of disbelief. Little, it seemed, had a back problem and a specialist advised Birmingham not to sign him.

Little takes up the story: 'Apparently I had a displaced vertebra which was causing a pelvic problem. Jim Smith was away on holiday and someone panicked a bit. So the transfer was off. I have never had the least trouble with my back before or since.'

The diagnosis, right or wrong, saved Birmingham City a fortune, for the next season was to be Little's last as a first-team player. On March 10, 1980, less than eight years after making his full debut, Little's knee went again. Ironically, the match was a minute from not being played on that Monday night, for West Ham had beaten Villa 1-0 with a last-minute goal in an F.A. Cup quarter-final at Upton Park and the replay was scheduled for that same night. How bitter the twist, too, that five days later Gray was to score the winning goal for Wolves in the League Cup final at Wembley.

'The knee went in a tackle about ten yards past the halfway line,' says Little. 'Next morning I tried to walk and the knee was like a big ball. It was hurting so much I couldn't move it.'

So began ten months of pain and despair, lit occasionally by a few days of hope.

'I remember time and time again willing myself to play in the reserves, going home to Heather who would have the ice packs ready to put on the swelling. Then the fluid would go and I'd try once more. She would say, "What are you doing to yourself?" But the game meant so much to me, I just had to battle away.

'I made the first-team squad a few times the next season. Finally I decided to give it one last go. I really pushed myself in training and in the end I couldn't even walk. That was it. I just had to finish. Mike Pejic, who had a pelvic problem, and I left at the same time, in February 1980. I was only 27 but I suppose I'm lucky in that I've stayed in the game ever since. I never thought I would but that's how it turned out.

'One of my big regrets was that I missed the championship medal. I was part of it and yet, in a way, I wasn't. I think I'd have enjoyed playing alongside Peter Withe, too. He was a bit like Keith Leonard, taking the flak.'

Little was granted a testimonial and later joined the Villa coaching staff, taking charge of the youth team. 'I believe in spending a lot of time on technique,' he says. 'When I was trying to come back, I played with some of the same kids. One of the things I hated was being picked for the reserves just because of who I was. It helped me make up my mind to go when I looked at kids like Mark Walters and I realised I wasn't as good as he was. I just couldn't go flat out and I knew I was blocking the progress of some youngster.

'Mark was a major talent. I thought he would set the world alight because at 15, honestly, he was the best I had seen. I still believe he can fulfil himself. Tony Daley was different, incredibly quick, and there were other good kids like the Aussie, Tony Dorigo, Darren Bradley, David Norton, Mark Burke and Phil Robinson.

'I believe Daley was taken away from me too early and, because of that, didn't spend enough time on techniques. Sixteen is too young and in the long run joining the first-team squad at that age slowed his progress.

Disagreements over Daley and one or two other matters led to Little walking out of Villa, then managed by Graham Turner. He joined Sammy Chapman at Wolves, controlled by the reviled Bhatti Brothers. 'After 12 years with Villa, the comparisons were untrue. Sometimes we didn't have a football, never mind kit. I did it for Sammy, certainly not the money because at times I wasn't paid at all,' he says.

When Chapman left, Little took over a club that showed all the signs of heading for extinction. Little's short period at impoverished Molineux was a minor success, his probity and wry humour appealing to players and public alike. It didn't stop him being sacked, however, and sacked to be replaced by Turner.

Most men would envy Turner his triumphs at Wolves, wondering perhaps if they might not have achieved as much in rebuilding the old club's reputation. Not Little, though. Honest as ever, he says: 'It was too early for me. At the time I didn't know enough about organisation, administration or management. I don't criticise the fella, he's done a tremendous job with Wolves. It's no good bearing grudges. I like to shake hands and get on with things.

'As a manager now, I try to enjoy myself. I keep separate from players but try to communicate. I don't know whether Graham was very good at that.'

So Little returned to the North to work with Bruce Rioch at Middlesbrough for three years, leaving his former Villa colleague to manage Darlington, where, after being relegated to the Vauxhall Conference League, promotion back to Division Four was achieved in a season.

Nevertheless, the West Midlands has not seen the last of Brian Little, I am sure. He says: 'I love it down there. I'd go back tomorrow and you know the first thing I would do if I wasn't in football — buy a season ticket for Villa.'

Brian Little

Born Durham City 25th November 1953. Debut 30th October 1971. League appearances 242 + 5, goals 60. F.A. Cup 15 + 1/4. FL Cup 29 + 1/15. Europe 8/3. Total 294 + 7/82. One England cap. F.A. Youth Cup-winners medal, League Cup tankards 1975, 1977. Second Division promotion 1975.

CHAPTER 7

Andy Gray

THERE ARE PLAYERS COMMITTED 100 PER CENT on a football field and few who gave, as former Villa manager Ron Saunders always demanded, 110 per cent. And then there was Andy Gray. He would have sold his car and re-mortgaged his house for one extra touch of the ball. Villa have had better players and bigger goalscorers but no fan ever doubted they had a greater trier or, because his enthusiasm and his lifestyle spilled generously into the outside world, a more glittering star. In Birmingham, Andy Gray was the people's footballer. Only Steve Bull at Molineux has had a comparable impact on the West Midlands public over the past two decades.

Yet, oddly, for all the adoration, the reminiscences of this Gray header or that Gray volley, the Scot from an ugly estate on the outskirts of Glasgow was never on the field to win a trophy with the team he admits to love best of the five he has played for. There is a tankard to show that Villa won the League Cup while he was their centre-forward in 1976-77, but on the day Chris Nicholl and Brian Little, two, scored the goals to defeat Everton 3-2 in a second replay, Gray was on the bench, injured.

Elsewhere, Gray won a League Cup tankard after scoring the only goal at Wembley when Wolves beat Forest 1-0 in 1980; League championship, F.A. Cup and European Cup-winners Cup medals with Everton in the two years before rejoining

Gray the Elder scores against Watford during his second term at Villa Park.

Villa in the summer of 1985; and perhaps, most tellingly of all, a Scottish League championship medal with Glasgow Rangers after being transferred by Villa for a second time. Not ten men have won both Football League and Scottish League championship medals. They are the manifestation of his talents but they are not the total.

Gray was, you see, the epitome of the self-made player, of will over skill, of courage over cynicism and of enthusiasm above anything. It was said a thousand times that he went in where angels feared to tread, and if this suggests there was an awesome quality about the way he threw himself at the ball, then I suppose it sums up his style fairly well; the blond, long-jawed Pict hurling himself time and again at a Roman wall of defenders, asking nothing and giving a good deal less.

He says: 'I was a player who gave heart and soul to everything I did. I have always been the eternal optimist, I don't have a pessimistic thought. I was never blessed with great skill but I had a great big heart and I knew I would always score goals. I couldn't dribble past half-a-dozen men in the area and score magnificently but I never let a defender forget I was around. I upset players and made a nuisance of myself. I remember when I came down to England, John Bond said I wouldn't last 18 months the way I chucked myself around. That was 17 years ago, so I think I proved him wrong.'

Gray's two periods at Villa Park were very different. From the day he joined the club as a £110,000 purchase from Dundee United to the afternoon he left to play for Wolves, at £1,469,000, he was Bonny Prince Charlie and Rob Roy and every other hero to be found north of the border. When he returned six years later, still only 29, the innocence had gone, the laughing buccaneer had matured with disappointment and triumph. He still bubbled with enthusiasm and love of the game, but with maturity came the inevitability that instead of making things happen, he was waiting for them to happen.

Today he admits, with characteristic honesty, that his return was a mistake. In 53 appearances, he scored 9 goals and, although it is true that he was rarely an out-and-out centre-forward, he grew more apprehensive in the penalty area the oftener he .played. Villa, too, were relegated and, distressed and vulnerable, he was hurt further when Graham Taylor chose to give him a free transfer within weeks of Taylor's appointment as manager.

There are many points Gray makes about the worst two years of his career but it would not be doing him justice to dwell on them at any length at this stage. Even now he will sadly tell friends that 'although that spell may not have destroyed my reputation it went a long way towards fans thinking that I was not the guy they remember.'

Well, we all remember him as a bubble-haired kid before he wore bristles on his match-day chin. Hustled down from Dundee United by manager Ron Saunders, he joined a team in transition — moreover, a team that was being remoulded on

Gray hails his first goal for Villa in front of the Holte End.

the hoof, for Saunders had led Villa to promotion and was moving out the older faithful — and one or two, like Steve Hunt, who had strong opinions.

More immediately, Gray was a direct replacement for Keith Leonard whose knee injury cruelly ended his career on September 13, 1975. Two weeks later, Saunders beat Schalke 04, of West Germany, to Gray's signature, and the 19-year-old made his debut on English soil on October 4 in a goalless draw at Middlesbrough. In that same team were Brian Little, John Deehan and John Gidman, all young and outstanding players who ought to have been the foundation of the League championship side of 1980-81. It is one of the less credible stories about Villa that they weren't, but it is a fact. This made Saunders more wizard than prodigal, although the second element was definitely present.

Gray enjoyed those early days. He was to enjoy his first full season even better. He became one of the sights of the First Division, a bird of prey to be seen before captivity. Alongside, Brian Little matched the suppressed fury of Gray's play with his own caressing touch, while Birmingham-born Deehan provided effort and strength as the season progressed. Between them, they scored 73 League and Cup goals which should have earned more for Villa than the League Cup, a sixth-round F.A. Cup knockout and fourth in the First Division.

Ten Little goals, two of them in the second replay of the final at Old Trafford, were the reason Villa won the League Cup but it was Gray's 25 in 36 First Division games which earned him the admiration of fellow players. He was practically uncontainable, from the first match against West Ham, when he scored twice, to the last against West Brom when he went one better and struck a marvellous hat-trick.

He has said that '76-77 was his golden year, spoiled only by two pieces of foolishness, one of which probably cost him a place in Scotland's World Cup team of 1978 which, in turn, proved an expensive misjudgment by national manager Ally McLeod whose team in Argentina so desperately required the sort of machismo to-hell-and-back qualities typified by the young Gray.

His first international cap came in December, 1975, but he had not really fulfilled himself with Scotland until his first goals in a 6-0 drubbing of Finland at Hampden Park. His next and fourth game in the blue shirt — a World Cup qualifying match against Czechoslovakia — can still move him to a sense of frustration. He reacted to an elbow in the face from his marker, the huge Anton Ondrus, by chasing him, spinning him round and flooring him with a right hook learned on the Drumchapel Estate, Glasgow. Ondrus played Hollywood on the turf and, after the officials had separated jostling players, the referee sent off both men. Scotland lost 2-0 and Gray was ready-made and parcelled as the guilty man.

Gray says: 'The sending off cost me a lot more than

The Scot in one of his
last matches for Villa
the first time around.

damaged pride. I was banned for three internationals but the
price was far greater than that. Effectively, it cost me a dozen
games including the following three World Cup qualifying
matches. Willie Ormond was replaced by McLeod as
Scotland's manager and I became the forgotten man of
Scottish football. I didn't feature again until after Mexico.

'The biggest disappointment of my career is never having been to a World Cup, not even as a commentator, believe it or not. I like to think I would have made a difference in Mexico particularly.'

A few weeks later, he was in more trouble. Incensed by Manchester United fans chanting abuse from their area at Villa Park, he delivered an expansive 'V' sign which was not only seen by the baying crowd but caught, full frontal, by a newspaper photographer. Villa won 3-2, Gray scoring twice, but the values being what they are it was Gray's two fingers and not his two goals that the paper headlined. He was contrite in front of an F.A. disciplinary committee who fined him £100, which in those heady days might have been his Saturday night champagne bill.

Gray and his Villa successor, Peter Withe, were two of the great onfield talkers, but where Gray often gestured his annoyance or engaged in repartee and dirty looks, Withe kept up a barrage of comment and long-suffering glares. They were both fairly consistently booked for tongue-lashing, yet they learned which referee would put up with how much and, most important of all, when to stop short of being sent off. Gray's learning process was greatly enhanced by the 'V'-sign incident. He vowed to control himself in future and by and large did so.

And so his wonderful season progressed. Saunders had acquired Dennis Mortimer from Coventry as well as the spiky Alex Cropley from Arsenal. This wee Scot was a football gremlin, sharp and combative, exactly the right type to fit in with the powerful Mortimer and Frank Carrodus, a brilliant athlete whose ground coverage, in Saunders' view, more than made up for his defects on the ball. The trio were a prototype Saunders midfield, remarkably similar in method to the Cowans, Mortimer, Bremner line-up of championship year. Indeed, when Carrodus was seriously injured in April, Cowans took his place.

Defensively, Villa were not quite so strong and when the late-season pressure on them increased, it was this area that

It's mine!

began to malfunction, a spell of four defeats in six matches ruining their title aspirations. There was, however, personal glory for Gray, although it was slightly stained by a decision of Saunders that can only be understood in the context of the manager's obsession with equal treatment to each team member. Some may call it envy, I am not sure.

The Professional Footballers' Association chose Gray as Footballer of the Year and Young Footballer of the Year, a double that can never be repeated because of new rules. As chairman of the PFA, Derek Dougan requested Saunders to allow Gray to travel to London to receive his awards. No, said Saunders, Gray was tired after Saturday's League Cup final and he needed plenty of rest before the replay the following Wednesday. Dougan's anger was tidal, a condition made worse by the fact that ITV were televising the ceremony. Saunders proved unbudgeable and club chairman Sir William Dugdale would not overrule his manager.

Dougan's next ploy was to ask Gray to give up the senior award to someone who could make the dinner! Not surprisingly, Gray told him where to put his suggestion and so it was decided to take the mountain of equipment to Mohammad. The presentation was made by Villa skipper Chris Nicholl to Gray in his own home and relayed back to the dinner, and the rest of Britain.

Gray says: 'Had I known what I know now, I'd have jumped into my car and driven to the dinner. I didn't realise what a prestigious occasion it was until I went the following year.'

The incident, I am certain, sowed the seeds of Gray's disillusionment with Saunders. 1977-78 should have been a great Villa year, the maturing of an exciting young team and an affirmation of Saunders' management talent. It wasn't. No sooner had it been created than he started dismantling it. Gray, Little and Deehan scored only 37 goals between them in a no-show season in League, League Cup and F.A. Cup. Only a sally into the UEFA Cup brightened the mood of the terraces

Gray as the fans love to remember him.

but by the time Villa travelled to Nou Camp stadium for a quarter-final date with Johan Cruyff and Barcelona, Gray's relationship with Saunders had ruptured.

Gray says the manager accused him of being 'chicken' and a cheat for refusing to play the return leg — the teams had drawn 2-2 at Villa Park — at Nou Camp. The slur bit deep, so deeply that Gray admits he has not forgiven Saunders to this day. 'It wouldn't have been fair to the rest of the team,' says Gray. 'I would have been no good to them. Of course, I'd have loved to play but it was hopeless with that injury.'

Saunders' remark was unwise, to say the least. Gray may have been a lively lad around the clubs to which his attraction was so great he actually started his own a year later. But he had absolute integrity and loyalty to football. With fame, too, came the self-confidence to make decisions outside football, some of them disastrous.

Anyway, Gray should have earned more respect from his manager for his willingness to turn out despite injury. 'I have played many games when I wasn't fit. People claim I am injury prone, yet my career has spanned 15 years and I have played more than 600 games,' he says. 'I reckon in 100 of those I shouldn't have gone on but I always regarded it as a compliment if a manager wanted me to play, anyway.

'In hindsight, I was stupid. Frequently I played with pain-killing injections and that could mean a delay in real recovery. The doctor would pump them into me and I would leave the dressing room hardly able to feel my legs. The injections wore off and I'd finish a match in agony. Since those Villa days, I have refused to take painkillers. Too many clubs want you to risk your future health. In a way, this is cheating, because spectators and your team-mates expect you to be able to give everything on the pitch, and you can't if you're carrying an injury.

'I could name you a team of first-class players who had to finish because they were abused so badly.

'It has improved in the first and second divisions because most clubs realise they're taking stupid gambles. Maybe my career would have lasted a wee bit longer had I been more careful in those days.'

Gray remains resentful of other aspects of Saunders' leadership. He has for a long time expounded the theory that

One of the many — Gray scores against Norwich.

Saunders could not or would not keep players who also became celebrities; that, in effect, he wanted 'yes' men. This, Gray contends, led to players with strong characters being discarded. Many were the times, too, when they were stopped from being interviewed by press, radio or television, allegedly in the interests of equality in the team.

Some of these criticisms are well founded. Players such as Gray, Nicholl, Burridge and Gidman were too outspoken for Saunders whose insecurity would show through in the oddest ways. But there can be no denying his record, no matter how ruthless he appeared to be to those with a more sensitive nature. Nor were Mortimer, Withe, Allan Evans and Kenny Swain shrinking violets, and each of them prospered under Saunders. There was between Saunders and Gray-Gidman a fierce clash of personalities — maybe wills, too — and in those circumstances a successful manager almost inevitably wins —

particularly if he has as sharp a political awarness and ability to manipulate as Saunders did.

So the season '78-79 was bound to end in tears. There were strong similarities in that Villa again went out of the F.A. Cup in the third round, the League Cup in the third round and were eighth in the League, although by then Gray was so disenchanted with Villa Park that he was on the verge of asking for a transfer. Before the start of the next season, he did so. Twice he was refused before, amid a riot of publicity, the Villa board decided to grant it, along with one for Gidman.

Gray tells of the day he and Gidman stood before the Villa directors, a group at least as split as a Wilson Cabinet, to explain why they wished to leave. The simple answer was 'Saunders'. Would they stay for more money, one director asked. Would they stay if Saunders went, dared another. Gray refused to answer, he says, on the grounds that he wouldn't stab a manager in the back in this way. So Saunders stayed to conduct an auction that had the football world agog.

Deals and counter-deals zipped down telephones. Saunders wanted £1 million for Gray and was prepared to swap him for Steve Daley of Wolves and £500,000. Enter Malcolm Allison of the insatiable appetite. He wanted Daley for Manchester City and, playing him like a large and hungry pike — smoking a large Havana cigar and wearing a wide-brimmed Fedora hat, at that — Wolves manager John Barnwell landed him with a bill of £1,150,000 plus VAT for Daley who never even played for England. Barnwell then paid £25,000 more for Gray and that was that.

Well, not quite. Saunders had been whispering behind his hand that Gray would never pass a medical examination of his injured knee and, sure enough, Wolves' club doctor reported serious doubts only hours before the player was due to walk out on to the Molineux pitch to be acclaimed as the golden future.

Barnwell, an engaging character himself, bluffed. He told his apprehensive directors: 'If you lose Gray, you lose a manager as well.' Gray signed, Gidman left for Everton shortly afterwards. Deehan was sold to West Brom, Little retired prematurely as did full-back Mike Pejic. And Villa won the championship the following season. Saunders' victory was total.

The story should end here. But while it might be said that current chairman Doug Ellis has made his fair share of enemies, he is also loyal to those who stand by him. Gray did during the late days of the Seventies when the Villa board disputes erupted in an elemental battle for power that was more like Dallas than dear old Brum. On one side were Ellis and Eric Houghton, director and former manager of Villa's last F.A. Cup-winning side, on the other the Bendall family faction. The Bendalls, whose fortune was based on liquidating firms, were supported by Saunders who, rightly I am sure, let it be known that Ellis would sack him if he won control. As fortune would have it, Villa were in an 11-match unbeaten run when the extraordinary general meeting was held in the Witton Lane stand of Villa Park. Ellis won on a hand vote but was beaten on the proxies, so he resigned and promptly sold his shareholding to the Bendalls.

Gray had actually departed by this time but when, at the end of the '84-85 season, Villa manager Graham Turner was looking for a centre-forward to replace Peter Withe, Ellis no doubt reminded him of Gray's feats with Everton, League champions, European Cup-winners holders and F.A. Cup finalists. Then Everton manager Howard Kendall signed Gary Lineker for Leicester City, and it was clear someone had to go. Gray, no doubt interested, too, in a sizeable signing-on fee, chose that it should be him.

Ellis followed up Turner's interest by flying to Portugal with Dave Ismay, a Birmingham comedian and friend of Gray's, to capture Gray's promise that Villa would have first option on his signature. PSV Eindhoven and Coventry City made him offers but he had been hypnotised again by the lion that watches over Villa Park from the main stand roof. True enough, Gray came in like a lion and went out like a lamb.

'I should never have gone back,' says Gray today. 'In hindsight it was wrong. I always said I would never do what Baxter and Stein did at Glasgow Rangers and come back after making their name and then leaving. But then your heart rules your head and you make these decisions, don't you?

'It had seemed such a golden opportunity and yet the two years turned out to be the most traumatic of my career. Everyone was so confident when I got there. Villa had done reasonably well the season before and I genuinely believed our squad would be pushing for honours. The crisis just crept over us. Suddenly we were languishing near the bottom of the table, every game was a struggle, I wasn't playing well and we were scrambling for our First Division lives.'

Gray had sound reasons for his early confidence. When he arrived, the squad included Steve McMahon, Mark Walters, Colin Gibson, Allan Evans, Nigel Spink and Gary Williams, all of them good-class First Division players. Turner, however, seemed to be searching for a missing link without quite knowing where it was missing. He sold McMahon and bought Steve Hodge. He sold Brendan Ormsby and bought Paul Elliott. He gave up on Gary Shaw and bought Simon Stainrod. He sold Colin Gibson and didn't buy anyone. The players hardly knew whether they were coming or going — and they showed it.

Perhaps I'm treating Turner harshly. Certainly his management record at Shrewsbury and Wolves have been excellent and it would require a careful search of League clubs to find a more genuinely reliable and hard-working manager. Villa happened to be his Devil's Island.

Gray says: 'Graham knows that he would have made different decisions if he were there again. There were players he allowed to go too soon but I wouldn't be over-critical and he is a much better manager because of his stay with Villa.'

After two wins in 22 matches, relieved only by a semi-final place in the League Cup, Turner splashed out on Steve Hunt and Andy Blair and, thereby strengthened in midfield, Villa inched their way to safety. Turner clung to his job through the summer, bought Martin Keown from Arsenal to bolster the defence and Garry Thompson from Sheffield Wednesday, presumably to supply the sharpness that Gray no longer seemed able to provide.

They made no difference. Villa were skidding further downwards and a 6-0 defeat at Nottingham Forest persuaded Ellis that he needed a change of manager. Turner went with dignity. A few weeks later, he replaced Brian Little at Molineux, overcoming initial abuse to rebuild a derelict club.

Turner has never uttered a word of criticism of Doug Ellis or Aston Villa, which is more than can be said of his successor, Billy McNeill, whose initial impact was quickly dissipated. Villa became a husk of a team, empty and dried out, blown to the bottom of the table. In their final 21 games from December 27, 1986, they won two, drew seven and lost 12. It was nothing less than disgraceful.

McNeill blamed Ellis for interference, a charge which Ellis denied. McNeill claimed Ellis picked up tales from players, especially Gray, and then threw them back in his face. Gray, in turn, denied it. My reading, as far as Turner and McNeill go, was that Ellis did get too close to one or two of the players but, equally, a manager should put a stop to that at the first inkling of it. Gray, I believe, suspects this was the reason Graham Taylor wanted him to leave Villa so swiftly.

Gray sums up the year in this way: 'Graham Turner wore his heart on his sleeve. When results were bad he would come in on a Monday morning looking depressed instead of bright and breezy.

'I still feel we had the basis of a good side the season we were relegated. There was certainly enough ability. I find it hard to understand McNeill's attitude, though. He didn't appear too bothered about the lads who were going through hell. It's not what you expect of a manager whose team are in the bottom reaches of the League. It still seems funny to me that Celtic sacked their manager for the first time in history and that McNeill left Villa and went straight to Parkhead. Coincidence? I don't think so, but maybe I'm wrong.

'When a team is doing well everyone bubbles. Badly, and there's sniping. A lot of "I'm all right, Jack" about. Subconsciously, people hide from the ball and playing becomes very difficult. That's when players are looking for help and guidance. McNeill would just come along for the five-a-side and go back to Manchester. That was it.'

The night relegation was certain, Gray, typically, went along to Ellis's house to console him. Ellis was sitting alone in state of abject dejection, for whatever his critics might say about him, the chairman's ego is indissolubly linked with Villa success. 'I didn't go along to blow my own trumpet,' says Gray. 'Yes, I would have liked to be manager of Aston Villa but that had nothing to do with going to have a drink with him that night. He had a raw deal from McNeill and, like me, he was in total despair. McNeill was going and I told Ellis what was wrong with the club. You could say we had a heated discussion. We are both passionate about the club and I told him a few things and I hope I helped him for the future.

'He wants success for Villa but some of the things he did were wrong. On the other hand, he has always allowed his managers to spend money and, contrary to public belief, never picked the team.

'No manager has been in a stronger position than when Taylor came in. I told Taylor that Ellis daren't sack him because he was Dougie's last throw.'

Andy Gray was first out, just like the equally extrovert Frank Worthington when Saunders took over at Birmingham City. 'I suppose he was a bit frightened because I was popular with the lads,' says Gray. 'I've heard it said that I had taken over the dressing room when McNeill was there. That wasn't true but I don't deny that I tried to help the younger players, particularly. No-one else was doing so.

'Taylor called me and told me I could go. I don't blame him, managers have to do what they think is right. My only criticism was his assessment of my attitude.

'He made the brave decision to weed out a load of players and get rid of them. He was correct in describing discipline as an absolute shambles.'

So the Andy Gray on Villa's books in the season of 1987-88 wasn't a fair-haired Scot but a black Londoner, signed from Crystal Palace. In a few years' time, no doubt there will be much confusion among the young statisticians.

For the Holte End, though, 'There's only one Andy Gray'. And always will be.

Andy Gray

Born 30th November, 1955. Signed from Dundee United £110,000. Debut 4th October 1975. Re-signed from Everton for £200,000 July 1985. League appearances 165 + 2/59. F.A. Cup 10/ 10 + 2/3. FL Cup 25/14. FL Members 1/0. Europe 5/2. Total 206 + 4/78. 20 Scotland caps (6 with Villa). Villa League Cup tankard 1977. PFA Player of the Year and Young Player of the Year 1977. Sold Wolves September 1979 for then British record transfer fee £1,469,000. Then Everton 1983, Villa, loan to Notts County, West Bromwich Albion and Glasgow Rangers. Also won F.A. Cup winners medal 1984, First Division championship medal and European Cup-winners Cup medal in 1985, League Cup winners tankard 1981 and Scottish Premier championship medal 1988.

Dennis Mortimer

DENNIS MORTIMER CHARGING DOWNFIELD WAS practically a force of nature, as much a sight of Villa Park as Bobby Charlton was at Old Trafford. There was something almost piratical about Mortimer's Dash, so much so that no-one would have been surprised had he appeared with a seadog's scarf — in claret and blue, of course — across his forehead and with cutlass advanced to chop his way through the enemy.

It is also fair to say that 'Morty' was the ladies' favourite at Villa Park. Darkly handsome and rather more sensitive-looking than the average footballer, he also, I was told many times, had by far the best legs at the club, a matter of total indifference to most of us, but to the girls who screamed as he set off on another of his brigand's charges, he was Harrison Ford breaching the Temple of Doom. The image is not the man, for Mortimer himself is intense, soft-spoken and devoted to his family, very much a product of a good upbringing in working-class Liverpool. And he was skipper of the greatest team Aston Villa ever put out, the League Champions of 1980-81 and the European Cup winners of 1981-82. The idea that he never played for England is still liable to cause anger among those who watched him grow from a very good player bought for £175,000 from Coventry City in December, 1975, into a supreme example of midfield style and industry by the time he raised the European Cup in the Feyenoord Stadium, Rotterdam, to the acclaim of all England.

Mortimer will be indelibly associated with those achievements and, because it is no accident that he has played in all but three of Villa's 32 matches in major international competition, this chapter will concentrate on the European Cup triumph, a year of football that was not only to witness great deeds but also the act of self-laceration that would inevitably lead to disintegration.

Ron Saunders, like Mortimer and Peter Withe, came from Liverpool. His list of dislikes was limitless. He demanded loyalty, even veneration. You were, quite simply, with him or against him. With him, and he could be generous and helpful. Against him, and he was at war, and clever he was at that, too, as opponents on the Villa board soon discovered. The fact that he happened to be the best manager Villa have had was neither incidental nor accidental. Saunders could show anyone how to run a club — his way.

He was not so much good with players as good with the whole team and his most recent successor, Graham Taylor, has gone on record to say that the club had not been run in the proper way since Saunders walked out.

Mortimer was his captain. The manager knew there would be absolute loyalty from him and he also knew that, while Mortimer would never stir up trouble in the dressing room, he would not be slow quietly to point out problems on the field and off it. This was language they both understood and, when Villa went through another of their turbulent boardroom periods, Saunders could be confident of player-support for the campaign to oust Doug Ellis from the board and present the unchallenged kingdom of Villa Park to Ron Bendall, whose knowledge of the game would not have filled a lace-hole.

An understanding of Saunders' methods is vital to Villa's most famous year, because the backdrop to a football style of withering counter-attack was a political joust between Saunders and his former boardroom friend, chairman Ron, and son and vice-chairman Don, that was to bring farce dancing into Villa Park, a grin of puckish glee on his face.

Mortimer escorted by the Villa doctor, leaves the pitch with only a few minutes left of the European Cup tie with Dynamo Kiev. Fortunately, the elbow wasn't broken and Mortimer was ready for the next round.

Villa's championship year — see the chapter on Peter Withe — was considered by Fleet Street to amount to a bit of a fluke. Forest and Liverpool were having off years, they implied, and Ipswich were a better side, anyway. Saunders did not like his work being treated in such cynical fashion, and neither did the team. Thus, justification of the championship was the chief motivation of the European Cup run.

After the defeat of Bayern Munich, Mortimer admitted to

me recently that he felt rather as Seb Coe had when, having retained his Olympic 1500 metres title in Los Angeles, he signalled with waving arms and teeth-clenched grimace to reporters who had decried his chances.

As champions, Villa served notice early on that there would be no repeat. Gary Shaw missed the start of the season and he and Withe were never the partnership of 1980-81. Two League defeats, one of them at home to Notts County, an away win at White Hart Lane and a sequence of six draws suggested that it was to be the Cups or nothing.

On September 16, FC Valur, a team of amateurs from Iceland, allowed Villa to ease their way into the competition with a 5-0 victory that should have been a good deal heavier. Withe and Terry Donovan scored twice each and Tony Morley rattled in the other in a match dominated by the Bremner, Cowans, Mortimer middle line.

Mortimer believes the draw had been perfect for his side. 'It was an easy baptism and helped us get over any nerves,' he says. 'It was early season and we weren't firing on all cylinders. It would have been difficult to face two matches with, say, Juventus.

'Afterwards, the Valur president was quoted as saying that the tie wasn't over yet and that he thought Valur on their home ground were capable of overturning us.'

This was football fantasy, the Icelandic equivalent of whistling to keep the spirits up — or cold out. Yet Mortimer and his team were well aware that there could be serious embarrassments in the return in Reykjavik. The possibility was quickly overcome when Shaw, back for his first full game, scored the first goal after 24 minutes, adding a second with a dipping 20-yard volley before half-time.

It was a performance in which sound professionalism was on display, for even the Valur president could not have asked for more from his weather. The wind was not only cold, it was gusting at more than 40 miles an hour. The pitch appeared to have been prepared under the hooves of a herd of charging

Middlesbrough beaten and Villa were on their way to the League title. Des Bremner and Colin Gibson are pictured behind the skipper.

buffalo. And then frozen rock solid. Villa flew back to Birmingham with deep relief. 'It wasn't only the wind,' says Mortimer. 'It was what the wind carried. There was a horrible smell of fish which got right into our throats. We couldn't wait to get away.'

If the first draw was ideal, the second was as hard as could be. Or almost. Villa avoided Liverpool, whose place in the competition was an automatic right as European champions, but were proffered Dynamo Berlin as consolation. The East German side had been good enough to beat Forest at the City Ground the previous season and, although Brian Clough worked a typical wonder by securing the tie on aggregate, there could be no doubting Dynamo credibility as a top continental side.

On October 21, in the shadow of the Berlin Wall, Villa answered the sceptics by defeating Dynamo Berlin 2-1 with two Morley goals that epitomised the economy of a Saunders side. Dynamo, with excellent players in Troppa, Reidiger and Ullrich, were the only side to score against Villa in the entire competition, yet even they could not have expected such parsimony from a team whose central defence had been, allegedly, disrupted by a long-term injury to Ken McNaught.

Fundamentally, Villa had two attacks. In the fifth minute Morley volleyed Shaw's header past Rudweilet — for which the translation must be Rottweiler, so hugely menacing did this property-guarder look against the bleakness of grey faces around him. Then, after Reidiger had equalised and Ullrich struck the post with a penalty kick, the Villa winger added the goal of his lifetime, running 70 yards from his own half, pursued by a pack of defenders, before shooting low past the giant in the 85th minute. The traffic of East Berlin practically stopped at that and Saunders was able to say later: 'We played as we intended. We soaked up a lot of preassure which we had expected because we had based our game on resolute defence and quick breakaways.'

Mortimer says: 'They were fit, strong and good on the ball, one of the outstanding sides in Europe at the time. The majority of them were over six feet tall and very physical, not in the sense that they tried to cripple us, but because they ran and chased everything. The referee gave a penalty for some obscure reason and we felt we didn't deserve that. Their guy hit the post and, when he followed up, Jimmy Rimmer stuck his foot out to his shot and the ball looped over the bar.'

It was typical of a side of Dynamo's dedication that they went to Villa Park with thoughts of making their bold game pay, and had they scored a little earlier than that goal in the 85th minute, they might have ended this chapter here and now. Mortimer admits he thought Villa were home and dry until that shot beat Rimmer. 'We suddenly realised that we were in jeopardy although Morley's second goal was our trump card. We held out but it was tense to the end. Even at this stage, we did not consider ourselves real European Cup contenders. The truth was that each victory was one in the eye for those who had doubted us.'

Mortimer scorns the misconceptions about Saunders, for

Bushy-haired Mortimer wins a heading duel with West Ham's Alan Devonshire in championship season.

now the captain's story inevitably shifts to the amazing dramas that were to unfold before the next round, two legs against Dynamo Kiev to be undertaken without the leadership of the man who, brought in by Ellis to replace Vic Crowe in June, 1974, was to walk out after a bitter row with Ron Bendall, his recent ally. Such are Villa Park politics.

'People get the wrong impression about Ron,' says Mortimer. 'They seem to think he ranted and raved but he wasn't like that at all. He was a quiet person on and off the field, so much so that I don't think I ever heard him raise his voice. He was either liked or hated but he was always respected. If you were prepared to do the job he asked you to do, life could be easy. He would think about you and help you.

'On the wrong side of him and it was trouble. He wasn't prepared for indiscipline or the wrong sort of discipline. As the results tell us, Ron's sides won.'

On one occasion they didn't and that occasion transformed the club. 'We won the European Cup but, really, the club was going downhill from the day he left,' Mortimer adds. 'There's still a great mystery as to why he went. I only had an inkling of his problems on the morning of the afternoon of the final dispute. He rang me to say he had problems but I was not to worry because he loved the Villa job and had no intention of leaving the club. Then he called again at 6 pm to say he had resigned. A lot had happened in eight or nine hours. It was a big shock and it will remain a mystery until he writes his autobiography.'

The day in question was February 9, 1982. Saunders, beside himself with anxiety, collapsed from influenza and exhaustion during a session at Bodymoor Heath the club's training campus. He went to Villa Park for his momentous interview with Ron Bendall, a huge, de Gaulle-like figure notable in his schooldays, remembered a classmate of his nearly 60 years later as 'a chess-player and a bully.' Saunders left Bendall's office checkmated and mentally beaten-up, no longer manager of the champions of England.

Bendall followed, commenting: 'As far as I am concerned there is no way the club is liable to pay compensation.' It was an important clue as to the causes of dispute, for the disagreement between Bendall, the financier and receiver, and Saunders, who put immense store on personal financial security, was about money. For months there had been a simmering row over Saunders' contract, an unusual one in which the manager would always receive three years of

Celebrations!

compensation if he was sacked. Bendall had arbitrarily told Saunders the contract was no longer 'roll-over' and that he was now working the last three years of a ten-year deal.

He interpreted Saunders' action in resigning as that of free will and, therefore, there would be no compensation, though I believe he changed his mind and Saunders was paid about £100,000 on the understanding that he did not talk publicly about the affair for a year. Saunders promptly joined Birmingham City and forfeited much of the sympathy of Villa fans. The postscript is intriguing, for practically on his deathbed eight months later, Bendall sold his entire 42 per cent shareholding for £500,000 to his second greatest enemy in football, Doug Ellis. I have often wondered if this was done to prevent Saunders from returning to Villa, as well he might had Bendall sold to a long-term sparring partner of Ellis's, Harry Parkes.

Bendall's benediction fell on Tony Barton, Saunders' knowledgeable assistant manager whose modest manner was liked by the players, and Roy McLaren, the first-team trainer.

Mortimer agrees that the greatest tribute to Saunders' management skill was that at this time of turmoil the discipline he had instilled in his staff was exactly the quality that prevented widespread dissension. 'The Eurpean Cup helped enormously, as well,' says Mortimer. 'The players had the character and determination to know that managers come and go and we are paid to win football games but, even so, had it not been for the European Cup it could have been different. There might have been discontent but we had a goal to aim at and we weren't going to chuck that away.

'I don't think any of us believed we were anything but Ron's team. He made us what we were and Tony was not really suited to the managerial role. He had a good insight into the game and he had compiled reports on the opposition so we knew what we were in for, yet nothing particularly changed in the club. The players pulled Villa through.'

Mortimer carried out his part as peacekeeper with impressive sincerity, always prepared to try to explain and always giving credit to his team-mates. As captain, he was focus of national attention and not an undiplomatic word crossed his lips and, incidentally, on this matter, still doesn't.

'As far as I am concerned, being captain just means tossing the coin. By my definition, professionals and captains are the same, they both lead by example. They give 100 per cent to every game. I suppose in one way, if my standards as captain had slipped, others may have followed but the lads were too experienced to contemplate that.

'Another misunderstanding was that Ron Saunders had big team talks before matches and that he would blow up at half-time. That didn't happen at all. Ron never called the team together to discuss tactics. He might have a word with a player about how to combat someone but he believed in getting our game right, not in thinking about the opposition. He had a good side and he knew it.

'As a psychologist, though, he was brilliant. It's fair to say that Tony Morley was never again the player he was at Villa in

Sunderland opened up for a Mortimer drive at the beginning of the 1982-83 season . . .

those days. He had his own way of treating Tony. When he scored, Tony would turn to the dug-out and signal as if to say 'there's your answer' and Ron would give him the V-sign. Sometimes I had the feeling that Ron believed he could make a player out of anyone but with a number it didn't work. Mind you, he got rid of them quickly.'

Mortimer undervalues his captaincy. On the pitch he was the standard-bearer. leading his men into battle or defending behind the stockade. But, while Cowans scurried the width of the field and Bremner ran tirelessly up and down the right-side, Mortimer directed with ball and keen intelligence what the tactics were to be. He had the coolest head on any park, and to see Mortimer panic was to see the first Martian land. Occasionally, his dispassionate approach was breathtaking. In the changing room after Villa had won the European Cup and, bearing in mind that the battleship *Coventry* — his first club — had just been sunk in the Falklands War, I asked him:

'Morty, is there something you would like to say to the lads in the Falklands?'

'I don't think it will mean much to them.'

'But, victory in the European Cup! It will mean a lot to the troops.'

'They'll hear it on the radio and I'm happy if they're pleased, but it doesn't really mean anything. That's a war. This is football.'

Yet the still waters are exceedingly deep. From Ron Saunders he learned an honesty about football that some players find uncomfortable.

And so to a place called Simferopol, an industrial town close by Sevastopol on the Soviet Union's Black Sea shore. It was here that the main battles of the Crimean War were fought and, judging by the number of soldiers shoulder-to-shoulder around the playing surface for the March 3 match with Dynamo Kiev, another was due any minute.

Villa had been diverted to Simferopol only a few days before the first leg of their quarter-final tie against Kiev, because the Dynamo pitch was frozen. Supporters from the Ukrainian capital were carried in their thousands the 200 miles to this open-air stadium set in a town which appeared to have no traffic problem because there were no cars, and roads of impacted mud.

After landing at an airport without radar — the pilot dipped below cloud level, a stewardess told us, to check that the airport was there — and being informed that they had been transferred from what approximates to a luxury hotel in Yalta into what approximated to a hotel, Villa began to wonder if they were the latest victims of a Soviet dirty tricks department.

Barton, on trial as a manager, confronted the Soviet authorities who shrugged their shoulders at the so-called horrors inflicted on their pampered Western guests. There was an absence of hot water in many rooms. Jimmy Rimmer's bath

'I'm in charge here' — a typical challenge to the opposition.

had a crack across the middle and the meat came, probably, from one of the horses the Light Brigade charged so gallantly into the jaws of death. Instead of being roughed up, Villa got tough.

They overcame the loss of Allan Evans from the centre of defence by using Bremner as the now-returned McNaught's foil. Bremner's task was to mark Blokhin, whose reputation as a kind of Communist Cruyff did not seem particularly exaggerated when he struck a post after four minutes.

Thereafter, Bremner kept tightly to him and the 40,000 crowd pressed behind the Red Army sentries had only fleeting chances to cheer. In Villa's single second-half breakaway, Shaw struck a post, and if Kiev did not know before, they realised that this English team was badly under-rated.

Dynamo manager Valeri Lobanovski said: 'I was impressed by Villa. They were more skilful and better prepared, although we obviously suffered from having little top-class competition in recent months.' Two weeks later, Villa completed the job with an early goal from Shaw and a 41st-minute header from McNaught settling this quarter final by half-time. Mortimer was swashbuckling in finest style, helping to block Blokhin as well as to set up a succession of attacks in a performance that made him believe seriously that Villa could become European champions.

With two minutes to go, however, he fell awkwardly after a tackle by Demyanenko and, so serious did his elbow injury seem that his arm was strapped to his side even before he left the pitch. 'It was a displaced elbow joint,' says Mortimer. 'I slipped and, as I fell heavily on my hand, the elbow gave way. The worst time was going to hospital because I was stuck for an hour in a traffic jam in real pain. Fortunately, it wasn't broken and I was okay to play in the semi-final at home to Anderlecht on April 7.

'People often say that a semi-final is harder than a final but I find a quarter-final is the worst. In a semi there's so much to play for and there's a chance of someone freezing. No-one freezes in a quarter-final so you know players are going to be at their peak. That's why Ken's goal was so important at Villa Park. It demoralised Kiev who were every bit as good as Berlin, strong and fit.'

Anderlecht went to Birmingham for a draw, despite their European knowledge that Villa travelled better than they hosted. Then, in the 27th minute, Cowans and Shaw shuttled superbly down the left and made room for a slashing Morley shot which rolled in off Munaron's far post. The Belgians sensed that another Villa goal and the tie in Brussels would become almost formal.

Armed with an offside trap of Panzer precision, they caught Villa out 18 times and gradually increased their tempo until Rimmer was called on to make a succession of outstanding saves.

'They could quite easily have won,' says Mortimer. 'As it happened, we were happy with the result because we were always stronger away from home. We knew that in Brussels they could not afford a mistake and, in these circumstances, players often lose their adventurousness and become stereotyped, basically just playing their roles out. But it was true that the Villa Park result flattered us. It was at this stage, I think, that we really could believe we would reach the final — 80 per cent certain. I would put it as high as that.'

Yet in football the unexpected must always be catered for, although how on earth Villa could have allowed for the possibility of an off-duty soldier nearly spoiling the chance of a place in Europe's greatest club competition no-one knows.

The Emile Verse stadium in Brussels was badly under-policed on the night of April 21. Worse than that, supporters in the 38,040 crowd were either packed together or segregated by flimsy fencing. The 7,000-or-so Villa fans were subjected to shocking abuse and the reaction of a number of youths, clearly unhinged by drink, was predictable. The crowd behind Rimmer's goal heaved and swayed as fans fought and police tried to act as a human barrier.

The game was only 27 minutes old when a soldier from the Sherwood Foresters, stationed with the British Army on the Rhine, ran on to the pitch and lay on the penalty spot in front of Rimmer's goal. Referee Dusan Krchnak held up play for six minutes for peace to be imposed and, eventually, a defensive campaign ended in a goalless draw. Anderlecht were quick to appeal that the delay had 'psychologically affected their players' and demanded of UEFA that Villa should be dismissed from the competition and their place in the final in Rotterdam on May 26 be handed to them.

Mortimer has characteristically down-to-earth views on the incident. 'I can't say I blame the lad for running on to the pitch. Someone was after him and there wasn't any other refuge. The police were just hitting out at any target around. Generally, our fans' behaviour was exceptionally good. This was the first real chance a lot of them had to see us away in Europe, and anyone who could make it did.

'As for the appeal, I think that had Anderlecht been about to score when the interruption came they would have had a case. But it wasn't like that, they were in the middle of the field. Even so we were nervous about the UEFA verdict.'

The Bendalls asked former Minister of Sport, Denis Howell, a Villa devotee, to represent them at the hearing. Howell, a Football League referee in the past, won the club case with one simple question of the referee: 'Where did you order the bounce up when play was resumed?' Krchnak, a Czech, replied: 'In midfield'. And Anderlecht's European Cup campaign ended. It was no consolation to them that Villa were fined £15,000 and were ordered to play their next European match behind closed doors.

Howell and secretary Steve Stride then worked intensively to ensure that Villa fans behaved themselves in Rotterdam for what was to be a final charged with drama and the stuff of dreams. The Birmingham MP still believes, incidentally, that the club's arrangements for fans at the final were so comprehensive that they should become a working model for the future.

Bayern Munich, boasting international players of the quality of Breitner, Rummenigge, Augenthaler and Hoeness, had won their previous dozen Cup finals and, from a visit I made to assess them, firmly believed they would return the huge high-shouldered trophy to Munich.

A fork of lightning greeted the players as they stepped out but that was nothing compared to the shock that was to await Villa. After 11 minutes, Rimmer signalled that a ricked neck was impeding his movement and forlornly left the field to be

Early days find a moustachioed Mortimer at Villa Park.

replaced by Nigel Spink in only his second game for the first team. Spink immediately plunged to Durnberger's shot in front of the right-hand post and, confident after this, became the night's central figure.

Mortimer comments: 'Nigel played a tremendous game but none of us were bothered for a moment when he came on. It was just one of those things we could do nothing about. It was a hell of an achievement to beat them that night. They were far more experienced than us and that is very important. I was the only player on our side who had ever played in a big final, and even then the Milk Cup was nothing like this one. We had hardly any internationals and I think many of us felt in our heart of hearts that we had justified the championship by reaching the final.

'We knew we could win but they never really allowed us to play. We just had to keep plugging away, trying to deny them as much space as possible. Had we gone to extra time there is no way we would have won. Even if Rummenigge's offside goal had stood, that would have been it. Foreign linesmen sometimes miss decisions like that one.'

'Plugging away' eventually brought the 67th-minute winning goal. Morley took Shaw's pass past Augenthaler with a hip wiggle, ran to the left by-line and crossed to Withe who, alone before a gaping goal, sidefooted the ball against a post from where it rolled over the line. I remember counting off every second of the final 13 minutes and, as I wrote at the time, the 43 seconds of injury time seemed like 43 years.

It was as if ice — although admittedly warming ice — was flowing through Mortimer's veins as he walked reflectively alone towards the VIP box where he was to receive the cup. Barton wept on the halfway line and the rest of the team jigged exultantly among the Villa fans.

'It was the greatest moment of my career and I wanted to get my hands on the trophy, I could see it up there gleaming in the floodlights, and the lads would not leave the fans,' he says. An official asked me to call them over and I said, 'I am, pal, but they can't hear me in this commotion.' When I finally held it I felt sheer exuberance. And then I thought of Phil Thompson, the Liverpool captain who had raised it so often before. I was a lad from Kirby, the same school as him. I am too down-to-earth to get wrapped up in celebrations but I was in a bit of a daze for a while afterwards. It all just mattered to me in my life, that's all.'

Morty claims the European Cup.

Half of Birmingham couldn't believe it, the other half didn't want to — Aston Villa, champions of Europe. There was a chance to launch the club to greatness but, instead, it fell apart. Soon after Barton had been sacked nearly two years to the day after he had wept for a very different reason, Mortimer and Bremner were told by Graham Turner, the new manager, that they were too old and had to move over. These two great

Villa servants joined up a year later at Birmingham City but the music had died.

Mortimer played 404 times for Villa and, as I say, never for England. Why?

'I think my best chance came in the season with Coventry before I joined Villa. Don Revie picked me for his squad in a testimonial match but I had to cry off because there was a Coventry fixture. Part of the reason for moving was that it would assist my England chances but within three games I was injured for eight weeks. I was playing consistently again by the time we won the League Cup in 1977 but there were some very good midfield players around at the time, men like Curry, Francis, McDermott, Hoddle and Wilkins. It just wasn't to be.'

Nevertheless, his place among the Villa Greats is assured for all time. There was never a player Villa fans admired more. Honesty was his byword, and theirs for him.

Dennis Mortimer

Born Liverpool 5th April 1952. Signed from Coventry City £175,000. Debut 26th December 1975. League appearances 315 + 1, goals 31. F.A. Cup 21/1. F.L. Cup 38/2. Europe 25/2. Total 403 + 1/36. England B Youth and under 23 caps. League Cup tankard 1977, First Division championship 1981, European Cup 1982, European Super Cup 1982. Over 600 first-class appearances with Coventry City, Villa, Brighton, Sheffield United (loan), Birmingham City.

CHAPTER 9

Peter Withe

FOR 'THE LAST PIECE OF THE JIGSAW', PETER Withe was a mighty handful. Indeed, for opposition defences, strikers don't come more inconvenient than this fourth son of five children from Liverpool. It was his presence that in one season directly led to an average First Division side becoming championship material, for the man with an eagle glint about the eyes was the central figure of strength and authority for whom Saunders had long been looking to complement the visionary passing of Cowans, the tricky wing-play of Tony Morley and the cunning touches of Gary Shaw.

Withe was already 29 when he decided to join Villa rather than Leeds or Everton, the club he had supported devotedly even on his travels around the more northern byways of English soccer. His two years with Newcastle United in the Second Division had been educational rather than triumphant, but Saunders had seen him lead Forest with such tireless enthusiasm that, old centre-forward as he once was, he knew his man and how to get him. For all his reputation as a 'sergeant-major' of a manager, Saunders could turn on the manly charm with such effect that a chorus of 'Kiss Me Goodnight, Sergeant Major' would never have been inappropriate.

Peter Withe, a scrubland of beard on his lower face, straightbacked, rangy and an addictive talker on the field, was just as independent and, I might say, even more fearless than

Peter Withe and an admiring ballboy share his goalscoring joy.

his bosses, who have included Saunders, Clough and Bill McGarry. More concisely, he is his own man: determined, helpful and utterly a slave of his word.

I have seen him hurt, furious at what he considered an injustice: I have seen him retaliate, make enemies, rough up defenders and curse the whole world. But I never saw him flinch or surrender.

Confronted with one of his sins, he would raise an eyebrow, smile knowingly or crack an impudent joke. And he had a wonderful Liverpudlian eagerness about him.

Villa supporters loved him, too, for his little acts of showmanship. At the end of each match at Villa Park, he would trot to the far corner of the Holte End and collect a bag of sweets from an admirer, clutching them like a happy little boy as, waving to the stands, he headed for the showers minutes after his team-mates.

He thinks quickly, too. Before the penultimate match of championship year, the players were discussing their opposition, Middlesbrough, bemoaning the fact that they were Villa's bogey side. 'Funny,' said Withe, 'in all my career I have never been on the losing side against Middlesbrough. It's just one of those things.'

He recalls: 'You should have seen their expressions. We could have had ten but settled for three. In one 25-minute spell they couldn't get the ball out of their half. I hit both posts and the bar.

'Afterwards, the lads congratulated me on keeping my unbeaten record. Well, it was rubbish, wasn't it? I had just made it up to get them in the mood. A little white lie like that doesn't come amiss.'

Just as the 1977 League Cup will be remembered for Brian Little's sparkling contribution and the European Cup for Dennis Mortimer's, so the First Division title brought all of Withe's special qualities to the forefront.

He was the eagle who landed at Villa Park, predatory, avaricious for the ball, the man his colleagues looked for first. He was always being called 'a typical old-fashioned England centre-forward' but he wasn't. His style was a modern phenomenon — the target man — who could act as a decoy, or like one of those hay-stuffed dummies army recruits stick their bayonets through, the heavyweight who takes stick.

Saunders knew just how to use him. Cowans-to-Shaw-to-Withe for a knock-down was as common at Villa Park as the grass itself: Cowans-to-Shaw-to-Morley for a cross to Withe in the penalty area just as much so. By then Gary Shaw was becoming a forward with sting, his one-touch passes a feature of the First Division. On his day there wasn't a better winger in the country than Tony Morley, capped six times by England but always an enigma — even, I suspect, to himself. Morley had speed, balance and a fine sense of where danger could be created, yet he needed constantly to be goaded, a task for which Saunders was supremely capable.

The Villa centre-forward had a special relationship with referees. This one appears to be going cross-eyed in disbelief.

In all, Villa used just 14 players in the championship season, a wonderful bonus for any team and an amazing contrast with the previous season when they employed no fewer than 29. After a summer of long knives, Saunders concentrated on players in whom he had total faith, even when, as in the case of Cowans and Morley, they badly lost form.

As Withe says, the team had a strong backbone, Jimmy Rimmer in goal, Ken McNaught and Allan Evans centre-backs, Cowans and Mortimer in central midfield and himself at the front. Of the six, five were ever-present, Withe himself missing six matches in three of which Villa suffered defeats. Kenny Swain and Morley also had 100 per cent records while Shaw missed two.

Withe remembers incidents with a clarity undiminshed by a decade. His first goals of the season, indeed his first for Villa, came in a 2-2 draw at Maine Road on August 23. 'The opener I brought down with my chest and volleyed,' he says of a characteristic Withe effort. 'The second was a header from a free-kick. We were two-up and Manchester City came back to draw 2-2. That season was funny because what with the transfer and moving my family to Birmingham I didn't have time to keep my fitness as I always had. I went back to pre-season training but for the first half-dozen matches I wasn't at my peak. It was a different kind of football, too. I got battered to death in the Second Division. It was much harder physically, and after having been down there I wanted to prove I was still good enough for the First Division.'

Withe's story of the first title to come to Villa Park in 71 years begins much earlier, in a soccer-daft household where the four boys vied to turn at least semi-pro like their father. Peter played in his school teams and had a couple of trials with good non-League clubs. If the spark wasn't there, it had to be found elsewhere and so he was packed off to the docks as an apprentice electrician at the age of 14, attending college once a week. It was not until his 20th birthday on August 30, 1971 that he finally threw away his snap-box and became a professional footballer, swapping 12 hours a day at the docks for morning training and the Saturday afternoon game.

'It was always on my mind to be a professional. A former Everton player, Peter Duffy, kept going on at me about it but I had two brothers who had been given trials and got nowhere. Finally, I went to Southport. I couldn't believe it at first. I had

Chelsea's defence rooted to the spot as Withe takes off to score in a 1984 game.

played football every day of the week, matches on Wednesday, Saturday and Sunday, sometimes two on Sunday, and there I was about to be paid for it. In at 10 a.m., finish at 1 p.m. and a Saturday game. It was one extreme to the other. I thought "this is the life for me".'

The great thing about Withe was that each year he improved noticeably. From Southport he went to Preston and then to Barrow and it seemed he was destined to be a toiler around the lower divisions or even out of the country, for he went to South Africa, playing for Port Elizabeth City and Arcadia Shepherds before Wolves, on the advice of Derek Dougan who had spotted a touch of 'the Doog' about the lean and inexhaustible six-footer, signed him for £13,500.

It was at Molineux on a couple of his few appearances that I first saw him and although the similarities with Dougan were clear, the likeness was as much negative as positive. Neither of them had a real turn of foot or scored with the frequency their effort warranted. Yet a closer look revealed that at this stage

Withe was Dougan without the aura of flamboyance. This was to emerge gradually, as did the Dougan-like ability to hold off opponents in the air as well as on the ground, to shield, to use the ball capably, to make space for team-mates and to be acutely aware of his own role. Withe would never be as spectacular as Dougan but, in the end, he would be just as valuable, his courage of a more earthy texture.

Withe puts down his late development to one factor: the amount of early professional grounding. He mused: 'I didn't have three years as a young pro and a lot of fundamental things passed me by. I was 22 at Wolves but really I was just a raw lad. Fortunately, I am a quick learner. I am also a fitness freak. I could run all day and, what's more, I wanted to. That's why I got better and better. I was gaining experience to be a leader of the line. Whoever had the ball, I would be the first man they would see. By the time I reached Villa I was the man to be hit nine times out of ten. If I could pop in a few goals as well, okay.'

That is a target man's code. And, for me, Withe was THE TARGET MAN. They come no better, as England managers Ron Greenwood and Bobby Robson were to recognise, the last of his 11 caps being awarded at the age of 33.

From Wolves, Withe went to Birmingham City who sold him to Forest for £42,000 — £8,000 less than they paid. Withe won his first championship medal with Clough but had been sold to Newcastle United for £200,000 by the time Forest won the European Cup. His move to Villa came two years later.

His story is: 'I had signed for Bill McGarry, my old boss at Molineux, on the understanding that I would re-sign only if we were promoted to the First Division. He tried to persuade me to stay with a very good contract at the age of 29 but money was not the most important factor. I still had ambitions and with freedom of contract coming in I took up the option to move to another club.

'There were six or seven clubs after me: two from London, two from abroad, and Leeds, Villa and Everton. Now Everton

A whiff of something powerful in the air as Withe and Mark Hughes of Manchester United go for a high ball.

were my club. I had watched them since I was a kid. I used to sell programmes on match days outside Goodison, and my family took it as a foregone conclusion that I would join them. I went to Leeds, then I saw Ron Saunders. He felt I was the final piece in the jigsaw. Villa had just had a good run-in, finishing seventh after a disastrous start, and they had reached the F.A. Cup quarter finals. He said his one ambition was to win the title and left me to make up my mind. He put no pressure on me. I went back to Everton and it seemed to me they were a team in transition and unlikely to be in contention.

'My family and friends couldn't believe it when I turned down Everton. I signed for Villa in May and we had sorted out a house by the start of the season. Five years I was to stay, my longest time anywhere. That makes them a special club for me.

'Coincidentally, our first match was away at Leeds, Morley and Shaw scored in a 2-1 win. We just went from strength to strength from then on.

'Forest and Villa were very similar in style. Both were always looking to attack by hitting on the break very quickly. Clough had a strong backbone to the team, too.

'We had a great bunch of lads at Villa. We knew we were a good side but never really thought about the championship. We just wanted to go out there and win the game because if you thought that far ahead you could be frightened to death. It wasn't until the media coverage got really heavy in the later stages that we realised we were on the brink.

'As I said, I started a bit slowly. It wasn't until mid-October that I scored my first home goal, although not scoring has never really worried me. We had others who could pop them in: Shaw of course, Morley and Morty, Sid Cowans and Allan Evans all came through with a few.'

By the time the goal came, Villa were in a nine-match run that brought them eight wins and the first of two 3-3 draws with Manchester United. There has always been a special flavour about United v Villa, epic battles from which the crack of leather on leather echoes along the generations who inhabit the Stretford and Holte Ends. From one gladiatorial contest at Old Trafford — Withe, Cowans, a penalty, and Shaw were the scorers — Villa switched to another, more tribal affair with Birmingham City at St Andrew's, this one won with the help of another Cowans penalty.

The serial of success was beginning to rival 'Crossroads' in

Withe and pals at worship.

suspended disbelief until it ended, unsurprisingly perhaps, at Anfield where the reigning champions won 2-1. The first of the season's two crises was instantly on Villa, who, taking four points from the next six games, were proclaimed by most of the press to be on a slide back to anonymity. The 'not good enough' cries that motivated Villa in next season's European Cup were first audible at this time, but at the training camp on Bodymoor Heath the older pros knew the decline was temporary.

At these times, as Liverpool have shown for more than 20 years, experience is everything. There will be a point in any season where two or three players are performing below ability. Sometimes the rest of the team can compensate, at others the players have to keep discipline and continue to try to do the right things.

'Chances were still being created, that was important,' says Withe. 'Saunders was telling us that basically we were doing the same things we had done before and that we would pick up in due course. It was just a lean patch. I hadn't scored for two months. You learn, though, that sometimes you just can't put them in and sometimes you just can't keep them out. Those spells are often broken by a deflected goal or something odd.

'I scored again in a drab match with Stoke on Boxing Day at Villa Park. It was the turning point although it may have seemed the 2-0 victory over Liverpool — after we had lost in the Cup at home to Ipswich — was that.'

The first of three capacity crowds that season saw Villa master Liverpool's tactical game. A cold Saturday in January became red-hot with controversy as Villa, a goal up but being squeezed backwards, like wine in a press, by Liverpool's back four, burst through the hole created by Shaw's hooked pass. As Liverpool waited for an offside decision against Mortimer, the Villa skipper ran around goalkeeper Ray Clemence to settle the matter, Withe having put his side ahead in the first half.

Now Villa were skimming towards their target. For Withe, who, good Evertonian that he is, admits that he does not like Liverpool, there was a further delight three weeks later, a 3-1 victory at Goodison Park in front of rows of Withes. They might just have relented to cheer a goal from 'ar Pete' but were muted as Morley, Mortimer and another Cowans penalty seemed to confirm Withe's objective judgment in wearing claret and blue rather than blue and white.

Into March Villa went, toppling all around them before the temporary setback of a 2-0 defeat at White Hart Lane was followed by victories against Southampton, Leicester and neighbours West Bromwich Albion.

At Villa Park on the night of April 8 Albion had championship pretensions themselves and Villa were beginning to look strained as their rivals outplayed them for long periods. Ron Atkinson's team had some exceptionally talented players — Bryan Robson, Cyrille Regis, Peter Barnes were just three — and a sound defence.

Indeed, many impartial fans regarded Albion as the more attractive side, smoother-moving and with greater variety. What they lacked was devilment, and luck. It seemed likely

A study in absolute concentration.

nevertheless, that defences would remain unpenetrated, until Brendon Batson attempted a back pass only to find Withe. Tony Godden was caught in mid-area and Withe calmly chipped the ball over him for a goal that, with impeccable timing, brought Villa's closest rivals, Ipswich, to Birmingham for a match the country considered would decide on whose

shelf the League-winners trophy would stand. Villa lost it —
and to a side who made them look distinctly careworn.

Crisis No. 2 was at hand. 'I remember Eric Gates scoring
the Ipswich second with a 30-yard screamer,' says Withe,
'Shaw got one back but Ipswich went away with a 2-1 win and
we thought we had blown it.

'You don't have to be told how despondent we were. Then
Ron Saunders reminded us there was still a lot to play for. The
championship was decided over 42 matches not three, he
pointed out. We had survived knock-backs before.'

Five days later, Villa beat Forest 2-0, drew at Stoke 48
hours after that and then beat Middlesbrough on April 25.

Ten thousand fans, 12 players and staff decamped for
Highbury on May 2 believing Villa had to draw to take the title
back up the motorway. Once again they lost a crucial match
which turned out to be of little importance after all. But the
scenes of distress among their fans were reminiscent of
relegation as Villa suffered a degree of stagefright that
restricted them to the occasional pawing reply to Arsenal's two
knock-out goals.

Transistor radios in the claret-and-blue sea revealed,
however, that Ipswich, too, had frozen adrenalin. Three goals
from Bosco Jankovic in a 3-1 Middlesbrough win at Ayresome
Park meant Bobby Robson did not have the championship to
his name when he went to manage England shortly afterwards.

Strangely enough, Villa's fate in the Eighties three times
hinged on Middlesbrough results. In 1988, they were defeated
at home in the last game of the season, giving Villa automatic
promotion on the strength of a 0-0 draw at Swindon. Justice
was done, for Middlesbrough went up through the play-offs,
although they were relegated in 1989 just one point behind
Villa, who would have gone down with them had not West
Ham lost at Liverpool in their last match of the season.

Withe, called into the England squad for the first time the
day before the Highbury defeat, was named Midlands Player
of the Year on the Sunday. 'A spectacular weekend for me,' he
says.

The pain went away when Withe later scored his only goal for England, against Hungary in April, 1983.

Twenty goals in 36 League games made him joint top scorer with Steve Archibald of Spurs. Shaw scored 18 and Morley 10 and the average First Division home attendance was 33,641.

'I still haven't received the Adidas golden boot for being top scorer. Archibald got it but although I keep writing to the firm I have always drawn blanks. Every time I think about it I'm left with a bad taste. They have always given two when the top total is shared.

'It was a phenomenal first season for me. The one unfortunate thing was that Ron Saunders lasted only a bit longer. I found him very likeable, a strict disciplinarian but very fair. He's a Scouser like me with the same kind of wit, though his is drier.

'He really understood experienced players. I know some of the younger ones, like Cowans, Morley and Shaw, found him difficult but he kept their feet on the ground. I bet if you asked them today they would tell you they realise now why he did certain things they didn't like at the time.

'I wouldn't differentiate between Clough and Saunders as to who was best. Both were top-class men.

'The year before I joined, Villa had a lot of injuries and I know some people said it was the hard Saunders training regime that led to it. But fitness is often a matter of trial and error and some changes are made so that training doesn't bore the pants off you. I found the training there easy and I'll tell you what — as the season wore on Villa became stronger, so he must have had it about right.'

Withe made his debut for England against Brazil at Wembley ten days after Highbury. It would be untrue to say that his international career was more than average but there are reasons for this which have nothing to do with his ability.

He was a specialist player, and asking him to do other than lead the line with bravery, strength and determination was rather like requesting a bulldog to run in a greyhound race. What Withe did well he perfected but, willing as he was, he did not possess the speed or touch to trouble Continental defensive patterns without the support of the whole system. He, and others such as Arsenal's Alan Smith or Villa's Tony Cascarino, are orchestrators, not soloists.

Withe scored once for England; an important goal it was, too, for it helped England beat Hungary 2-0 and revived their chances of going through to the finals of the European championships.

'That was one of my great memories,' he says. 'Looking back, international players always remember the first cap specially. The weekend Villa won the championship, Saunders called in to see me. 'How do you fancy playing alongside Kevin Keegan against the Brazilians?' he said. It sounded pretty good to me. As it happened, Keegan didn't play. I was unlucky not to score that day (May 12). I hit the foot of the post and, oddly, the ball ran across the goal and out of play the other side.'

He was picked for England in clutches of games and became the first Villa player to be selected for a World Cup finals when Greenwood named him for the competition in Spain. 'I regret never playing,' he adds. 'It was a big disappointment. I feel I would have been useful against the

In goes the European Cup winner.

West Germans because my style would have upset a few
people. Tactically, the Germans were brilliant. They knew just
what they had to do to beat us to the punch. The irony was that
we were eliminated although we didn't lose a match and we
also played so well to beat France.

'I suppose one of the most satisfying things for me was to
be chosen again two years later, for the match against Turkey.'

By then, Withe was 33 and his career with Villa had only a
year to run. Graham Turner had taken over from Tony Barton
and although the former Shrewsbury manager dispensed with a
number of the old guard, Withe was very much his type of
player, bold and honest. Chairman Ellis and Turner felt that a
two-year contract was as much as they could offer. Withe
wanted three. He knew he was still extremely fit and could have
a vital part to play in spanning the generations. Equally,

Turner was aware of the accelerating ageing process of all footballers, and particularly those in the core positions.

Withe was not to be budged. 'Graham wanted me to stay and he had turned down a £200,000 offer from Bobby Gould to take me to Coventry. I wanted to remain with Villa but it had to be on financially acceptable terms. They never were, so I took a free transfer and moved to Sheffield United, I suppose because Ian Porterfield sold it to me as Ron Saunders had: a fresh challenge, fresh impetus, doing a bit of a Keegan revival sort of thing. But it was the biggest wrench of my football career. I have some fond memories of Villa, none better. I might even have been there still had things worked out differently.'

Among his souvenirs was one shared by only an elite handful of men — scoring the winning goal in a European Cup Final. As goals go, it wasn't much, although the importance of it has been both a blessing and a burden to subsequent Villa teams, so much so that I have been unable to spot a single photograph of it on the walls inside Villa Park.

Withe, however, paints his own vivid picture of the ten seconds at the Feyenoord Stadium on May 26, 1982. 'The move started with Gary Williams who played the ball up to Shaw. He took it to the left and pushed it inside the full back to Morley. I half expected him to find me but, instead, he showed his marker the ball — they marked man for man — went outside and then as the defender went for the ball, drilled in his pass.

'I have seen this on video many times but I still recall the moment as if in slow motion. I knew I had to make contact first and the ball would go in. I told myself to concentrate 150 per cent and then, just as I was about to make contact, it hit a divot and bobbled. I followed through and hit it with my shin. As soon as I had, I knew it was going in, although it went in off the post.

'It was the most momentous goal of my career.'

And the ideal note on which to finish an unforgettable chapter in Villa history.

Peter Withe

Born 30th August 1951. Signed from Newcastle United for £500,000. Debut 16th August 1980. League appearances 182, goals 74. F.A. Cup 9/2. FL Cup 19/5. Europe 22/9. Total 232/90. 11 England caps, first Villa player in World Cup finals squad. First Division championship 1981, European Cup 1982, European Super Cup 1982. Other clubs: Southport, Barrow (Port Elizabeth, Arcadia Shepherds, South Africa), Wolves, Birmingham City, Nottingham Forest (with whom he won another First Division championship), Newcastle, Sheffield United (July 1986 free transfer), (Portland Timbers), Birmingham City (on loan), Huddersfield.

CHAPTER 10

Gordon Cowans

BY SAVAGE IRONY, GORDON COWANS' FOOTBALL career was split in two by a criminal act that would have disgraced a Bolivian bandit. In Villa's pre-season warm-up match against F.A. America of Mexico in Zaragoza, Spain, on August 18, 1983, Andreus Manso smashed Cowans' leg with a kick designed to cripple. Even today this gentle-natured Geordie remembers with sickening clarity, the instant boot made contact with shin, and a long association with the England team circumscribed at a great loss to the man and to football.

'Oh, there's no doubt he went over the top at me,' says Cowans. 'Maybe he had no intention of breaking my leg but he intended me harm. And he knew when he jogged back into the pack of F.C. America players that my leg was broken. He couldn't exactly know otherwise, it was just hanging. For a fraction of a second before the impact I knew what was happening but I had committed myself. As I went up in the air, I could feel the leg wobbling and I was just concentrating on keeping it off the floor. Our physio, Jim Williams, ran towards me and I was thinking: 'Is that it? Or will I be okay?' Well, it changed my life.'

Six years later — half of a footballer's prime time — Cowans acknowledges that it was not until last season that he began to play again as he had before that shattering blow. In the meantime, he spent three years playing for Bari, an industrial city on the arid heel of Italy, and returned to Villa, the club who 17 years ago persuaded the stick of a lad to leave his Mansfield, Derbyshire, home along with his parents.

With his only English club, Gordon was to win the League Cup, their first Division One championship for 71 years and the European Cup. He was to serve four managers, become the best all-round player in the greatest team to come out of Villa Park and win nine caps for England. Had he been blessed with luck and more self-assertion he might still have been playing alongside Bryan Robson in the World Cup team last summer.

With the candour and modesty which make such a popular figure, 'Sid' Cowans admits his greatest failing to be 'lack of self confidence or even the arrogance of someone like Paul Gascoigne who doesn't give a damn about anything'.

I recall watching Cowans in one of his international appearances when it was apparent that the manager had instructed him to take all dead-ball kicks. I doubt if there has been a better player in the Football League at this but, anyway, after about 30 minutes England were awarded a free-kick 35 yards-or-so from Scotland's goal. Cowans was preparing to take it when Glenn Hoddle stepped forward and gestured him away. Cowans went, and many of his admirers mourned his lack of authority.

Never mistake this, however, for a lack of courage, physical or moral. Bony as a racing greyhound, he can practically be heard rattling his way around a football pitch, distributing the ball and tackles with equal vigour.

For a player with the coolness to drive in the magnificent televised goal that began the 6-2 rout of Everton at Villa Park last season, his scoring totals have been moderate, declining as the years pass again, I suspect, because of his self-effacing attitude. He wants to be where he thinks he can most help endangered colleagues, rather than at the glory end.

But back to that terrible summer of 1983. The previous season had been Cowans' best.He was rightly hailed as

A midfield clash.

Midland Footballer of the Year and the best midfield player within 50 miles of Birmingham, Bryan Robson having left West Bromwich Albion for Manchester United.

He then won his first England cap against Wales on February 23, performing with a degree of skill that would have been beneficial to England in the World Cup in Mexico.

Bobby Robson had been watching Cowans' progress for as long as he had his namesake's. Three years earlier, in Villa's championship year, the then-Ipswich manager described him as 'potentially the most complete footballer and midfield man in English football.'

It was shortly afterwards that David Sexton made him captain of the national under-21 team for a match against Rumania in Bucharest, commenting: 'He has skill, vision and a heart as big as a lion, which is deceptively concealed in his fragile frame. I knew he would set a perfect example to the other lads. He is the kind of player who inspires others with his efforts.'

Thus flattered, he had a stinker: a game so bad that his season slipped memorably into decline. It was then that Ron Saunders showed himself to be such an excellent manager and judge of character, for the Man Who Never Smiled named Cowans on his team sheet to the very last day of the season at Highbury where Villa lost, and won the championship at the same time. Cowans, the left side of the Bremner, Mortimer, Cowans combination, was the drier-up in front of the back four of Swain, Evans, McNaught, Gibson or Williams. It was a disciplined role and maybe it was also a straitjacket that Cowans was unable to untie until Saunders' departure.

Next season, Cowans was helping Villa to the European Cup but, mystifyingly, there was to be no World Cup under Ron Greenwood, who might possibly have misunderstood Cowans' refusal to join the under-21 summer tour as a lack of desire to play for his country. 'I never like turning down my country but I feel that a good long rest will be the best cure for my problems,' said Cowans at the time. He must have been very deeply depressed, indeed.

By then, Saunders had departed from Villa Park. 'We didn't really appreciate how good he was until he left,' says Cowans. 'There were times when I really hated him, especially at the hard training. It was killing, yet the club was run on the right lines. He kept our feet on the ground, if you see what I mean. Only with Graham Taylor did we return to the important principles.'

Cowans and Gary Shaw were the newer gems of Saunders's collection. Cowans-to-Morley-to-Withe-to-Shaw was as routine a commentary line as the rounds of a hand of whist. Shaw, a fair-haired Brummie with Tom Cruise good looks, was the teeny-love of thousands of girls in and around the city. Cowans was more the favourite brother. Shaw had one talent that set him apart, the ability to make one touch that cut to the heart of the game, either by delivering the *coup de grâce* or setting it up. Cowans had half-a-dozen, but none more than a drilling long pass, with either foot.

Cowans hooks out of the Villa penalty area.

Naturally enough, both were the subject of continual transfer inquiries and it was Saunders's way deliberatley to under-value them, particularly at after-match press conferences. It was said that Saunders couldn't — or wouldn't — manage stars but I am sure that his often sardonic comments were more to do with the strategy of keeping level heads.

Cowans and Shaw were reaching the upper realms of their talent in 1982-83. Cowans was a regular England player by the summer while Shaw accompanied Cowans and Nigel Spink on the international tour of Australia, but failed through injury to win a cap.

In Australia, Cowans wanted to find out if he was to become a Naples player. Telephone calls pursued him around the country and, with the offer of an excellent Villa contract also dangling before him, his feelings were in turmoil.

Tony Barton, Saunders's assistant who had taken over 16 months earlier, thought he had lost the financial battle towards the end of May, even if he had never spoken personally to the Italian club. Indeed, if Barton was in the dark, Cowans himself was never in full light. He knew from discussions with agents that he stood to make about £250,000 from the move and his fiancée, Jackie, was so convinced she was leaving her Streetly home she commented: 'He could not turn down an offer like that. I agreed right away I would go with him.'

A day later the transfer was a smoking ruin. 'It was a great disappointment,' he says today. 'There was a hell of a lot of money on offer. Villa promised me a testimonial and their contract was good but what Naples put forward was ridiculous. It would have set me up for life. How could I refuse? I had always fancied going abroad when I was quite young because it would give me a chance to rebuild a career in England.'

Cowans was the victim of a takeover in Naples that had undertones of the Montagues and Capulets. Guiseppe Benetto, with whom Cowans had been negotiating, was overthrown by Antonio Juliano and the new chief was quick to announce: 'Cowans has no contract. The immediate deal is off.'

So for a while, at least, he remained a Villa player and prepared for the Home internationals and the tour of Australia, still clinging to the hope that Juliano would be overturned by the Benetto faction, as he had before, at a meeting of shareholders. He wasn't, and two months later Cowans was in a Zaragoza hospital with a smashed leg. No more than three further weeks had elapsed when an apparently minor knee injury to Shaw proved to be the greater tragedy, the slow, lingering end of a potentially outstanding football career.

Shaw was tackled by Ian Bowyer in the fourth match of the League season. Shaw, I remember, was lying twisted on the ground and the Nottingham Forest captain stooped to help lift him in the way that old soldiers do as if to imply 'the kid's having you on, ref.' Metaphorically, Shaw never got up, for in the following five seasons he played 23 games for Villa, little patches of play broken by long sequences of operation-rehabilitation-training . . . and pain.

In three weeks, then, Villa, winners of the European Super Cup with a 3-1 aggregate over Barcelona, had lost their brightest prospects. Steve McMahon, recently bought from

Cowans in
England
tracksuit.

Everton, said, 'I came to Villa to play with them.' Even the purchase of Paul Rideout and the burgeoning of Mark Walters's skills would not dull the ache at Villa Park. The club was sliding. Fast.

For months, Cowans sat, hobbled on crutches or limped to train at Bodymoor Heath. To add to Villa's troubles, Des Bremner managed less than a third of a season in all; McMahon, for all his aggression and hard running, did not complement Mortimer and only a run to the semi-final of the League Cup relieved a season that saw just three away League victories, a sure sign that Villa's centre-half Ken McNaught had also departed to leave Allan Evans searching for a central partner. Evans remained six further seasons and one was never found.

'I should have stayed away from training sessions. I realise that now,' says Cowans. 'At the time I thought it was better to keep turning up, that time would pass by and I would soon be with them again. I wanted to be involved but I wasn't really. They were the worst times of my football career.

'I trained with weights and did all of the usual things. Eventually I was walking and then jogging and the time came to kick the ball. It should have been a big moment. Instead of that, I felt a dreadful pain the very first time. It's obvious now that it was too early. I tried just to keep the ball up but that hurt as well. When Jim Williams lifted my leg I could feel movement in it. The X-rays all showed that it had healed but it hadn't. The fact was that there was still a crack in the bone and so I had to go back into plaster. In the end I missed the whole season.'

In the summer of '84, Barton was sacked as manager and replaced by Graham Turner, from Shrewsbury. Chairman Doug Ellis had hunted England and beyond for a successor to a modest man of great approachability who had been prepared to stand up for the rights of a manager, as he saw them. Long-term, perhaps, Barton and Roy McLaren, his assistant, may not have been a complete answer — although that has been thought of a number of excellent partnerships — but they would certainly have shown sesitivity in phasing out players who had served the club so expertly. Barton had a heart attack shortly after his dismissal.

Turner made it clear that Villa were in a new age of management. The club was to be run by the manager who would be part of an executive team, headed by Ellis. No doubt Turner had his own opinions of such stalwarts as Bremner and Mortimer, but giving Bremner a free transfer with at least two years of good football left him and then totally excluding Mortimer, for whom the chairman had no liking, was hasty and ill-advised.

No doubt, he expected to extract more from Cowans and McMahon than he could, while the other truth was that the famous Saunders reservoir of young players was drying up. Darren Bradley, Alan Curbishley, David Norton and Ray Walker were never going to be midfield players of the highest calibre, so that Cowans, struggling desperately almost on one leg, was victim of his own eagerness to return.

Scoring against Watford.

'I was always rushing to be back fit,' he recalls. 'Turner chose me for the first match of the season and I was delighted. Nevertheless, I was limping, something I realised only when I watched a video. I thought I just had to accept that the leg would never get stronger and that this was going to be how I would play football until I had to retire. The season I came back I was only a shadow of the player two years before. On top of that, I feel the side was being demolished too quickly.'

Cowans had been a plaintive sight. The touch was still there but only at half speed. Tackles that had once been delivered with a chop as neat as a master butcher's now came cautiously, as if his sub-conscious recoiled at the memory of Zaragoza and Andreus Manso's leg-breaker. Not that Cowans ever opted out. He is too much a pitman's son ever to mislay his moral courage.

At the time, he refused to blame his injury for poor form: again he was too much the competitor to do that. But his team-mates knew and when, finally, Turner left him out of the side for the first time after 274 league appearances, retrospect tells us that the brief glory of the championship era had ended.

The 1985-86 season started without Cowans, for he and

Paul Rideout, a bustling young centre-forward bought by Barton, had been sold to Bari, of the Italian First Division, for £850,000 as a job lot. Even for Italian deals this was an odd one, served up by Gianni Paladini, a former boy footballer with Naples who, at 41, was licensee of a Birmingham bar called Boogies Brasserie.

I had tracked down this unlikely intermediary to his cane chair in the bar a couple of days before the agreement with Franco Janich, the Bari general manager, had been signed. The man who had come to England as a waiter was, indeed, awaiting the biggest tip of his life, for he had persuaded Janich to renew the interest in Cowans he had first shown as Naples coach two years earlier. Bari had been promoted and were, therefore, permitted to sign three foreign players and, not only had Janich liked the look of Cowans in an April game with QPR, he had also been highly impressed by Rideout.

Paladini reckoned he spent £8,000 of his own money in smoothing the way to the transfers. His investment was well rewarded. He made £50,000, and later told me that one of the conditions for being paid was that he signed a note accusing me of high treason against Aston Villa. An attempt later to use this was laughed off by my newspaper.

Turner, away on holiday at the time, had six weeks in which to move for fresh players. Andy Gray was bought from Everton for £200,000. McMahon left for Liverpool and was quickly replaced by Steve Hodge from Forest. Then Paul Elliot came from Luton and Simon Stainrod from Sheffield Wednesday. Only four of the European Cup team remained at Villa Park. This was demolition on a grand scale.

Before, briefly, joining Cowans in Italy, however, there are one or two points to be made about the next two years. The heart had been ripped out of the club because the chairman, Doug Ellis, believed that change was as easy to affect in the dressing room as it was in the commercial department. He put strong pressures on Turner, making it clear to the former Shrewsbury manager that there were certain players he should not keep. Turner was as inexperienced in dealing with such demands as his successor, Billy McNeill, proved to be.

In fairness to the dauntless Ellis, now one of the most dynamic pensioners this side of eternity, he has made a successful corporation of Villa and found, in Graham Taylor, a man of similar strength of character, although that similarity is the only one I can think of.

Ellis liked Cowans and was shrewd enough to understand that though the thin man was firing on a cylinder and a half, he might not be in a couple of years time. With this in mind, he shook hands with Janich on having first refusal should Cowans wish to return to British football, and stayed in touch.

So Gordon and Jackie, now his wife, flew to Bari knowing that at the end of his three-year contract, they stood to gross about £400,000. 'It was no secret about the money,' says Cowans, frankly. 'But I had always fancied going abroad for a spell. I felt the style would suit me and to an extent it did. It was a challenge to break down their defences. They don't want to take chances, preferring safety first and keeping possession.'

Within a few weeks of the season, Cowans had broken his leg again and although the damage did not compare with his Zaragoza injury, it was to have a significant effect on his initial impact and, indeed, on Bari's future. They lasted only a season back in the First Division, a singular disappointment to the two Englishmen who may not have enjoyed the irony that a season later their erstwhile club in Birmingham was also relegated.

Yet there is no question that the Bari fans adored their little 'Sid'; loved him for his impetuousness in taking a risk with his famous 'killer' ball, for his unyielding determination and his visible desire to do well for his paymaster. Gradually, too, the strength returned to that once-fragile leg. 'We love you, Sid,' said one huge placard when it was thought he would be leaving Bari at the end of his second season there, and fans demonstrated their admiration in the dozen-and-one-ways only Italians know how.

'They were brilliant to me,' he says. 'In some ways, we

were unsettled, moving house several times, and Jackie particularly missed home. The wives are often alone there because players spend three or four days in a hotel before matches. It's pretty boring for them, too. I have no regrets, though. Well, perhaps one. I benefited as a player. I became much more mature and perhaps I didn't try the killer ball so often. The disappointment was relegation because not only did it mean a lesser level of football but also staying in the First Division would have reminded Bobby Robson that I was around and maybe worth a place in his squad. It would at least have made a trip by him over to Italy worthwhile.'

It helps to know a little about the Cowans family to appreciate why, when Taylor flew to Bari to make an assessment, Gordon was passionately anxious to return to Birmingham.

He was no more than a sprig of holly when Villa's attention was first drawn to him, a representative of Newlands school, playing for the Mansfield district team.

Neville Briggs, the scout concerned, had been struck to superlatives by the wee lad's skill in midfield and was soon chatting to Walter, Gordon's father, who as a pitman had transferred from Durham to the north Derbyshire coalfields seven years earlier. Gordon was only 10½ years old but Walter knew he had fathered a rich seam of talent — he hadn't been 25 years down the mine to be ignorant of that.

Villa were determined that this one wasn't going to get away and they approached his physical education master to invite the whole school to Villa Park to watch Villa in the second match of their first-ever season in the Third Division. 30,856 people and Newlands school turned up to watch Villa lose 0-1. 'I don't remember too much about the game,' says Cowans. 'I know I was flabbergasted to think a club would go to those lengths to try to impress us. I suppose I was always going to join Villa from then on.' This surely then, must have been the first recorded case of using a mackerel to catch a sprat.

Five years later, in July 1974, the Cowans family decamped from Mansfield and Walter took over control of the Villa youth hostel, where his son, an apprentice, lived with a band of youngsters, including Colin Gibson, Gary Williams and Brendan Ormsby. Villa had some outstanding lads but none with the innate ability of the chap who hardly looked big enough to carry his fashionably long hairstyle.

Walter was more like a brother than a father and Gordon loved sharing hobbies typical of mining communities. Soon after Walter became club kit man, moving to Drayton Bassett, one of his racing pigeons won a £320 cheque for coming first in the Midland section of the Grand National. Today, he's a top-class greyhound trainer.

The young Cowans made his debut as a substitute at Maine Road on February 7, 1976, a match after Charlie Aitken changed for his 659th and last appearance in claret and blue. Gordon signed full professional forms a month before his 18th birthday on October 27.

Thus, steeped in the lore of Villa Park, Cowans took a phone call from Taylor in Birmingham to his Bari appartment with all the nervousness he had shown when Saunders told him to warm up against Manchester City 12 years earlier.

'He said he was coming to Italy to watch me,' says Gordon. 'It was very late in the 1987-88 season and I had thought he wasn't interested. Southampton had been over a few times and so had John Sillett and several others. It seemed I would be going to one of the others and then out-of-the-blue came this call from the boss. Chris Nicholl, the Southampton manager, came over at the same time, and it was left to me to decide which club I preferred. It wasn't a difficult decision to make.'

Taylor warned Villa fans not to expect to see the Cowans of pre-Zaragoza days. He was older and would not hare about as he had. Maybe this was a typical spot of Taylor psychology but I must say it left many of us baffled. Sid the Workaholic, hard training fuelled by powerful eating, would never in

English football be allowed to stroll about, striking wicked passes into vulnerable areas. The days of Johnny Giles being allowed to find room in front of his defenders had long gone. Even Cowans' special favourite, Liam Brady, had discovered that a peerless left foot and the mind of a command general could often be nullified by boys with the legs and lungs to dwell on him for 90 minutes.

Villa's return to the First Division had been superbly plotted by Taylor. With Cowans and Derek Mountfield to supplement the midfield and defence, at a combined cost of £650,000, the manager was confident enough to hope for a place in the top half of the table and a good run in one of the cup competitions. 'I would need to spend more than £2 million to stand a chance of a top six place,' he said at a post-match celebration at Swindon.

By the end of last season, however, Villa were hanging on to their First Division status with all the certainty of Harold Lloyd grasping the fingers of a 20-storey-high clock face. Expecting security, the fans were delivered a set of results that made them wonder about Taylor's wisdom not only in buying wingers Ian Ormondroyd and Nigel Callaghan but Mountfield and Cowans, too. The Taylor warnings about Cowans began to make a kind of sense as he waxed and waned, too often off the pace of the game.

The truth was more fundamental, however. Villa's uncertainties in defence cast a pall over the rest of the side, forcing Taylor to make all manner of adjustment with further unsettling effects. Strangely perhaps, it was the loss of the two players many regarded as the only successes of the season, Martin Keown to Everton and Alan McInally to Bayern Munich — at a combined sum of nearly £2 million — that was to act as an instrument for improvement. Taylor bought Paul McGrath and Kent Nielsen, persuaded Ellis to update the Villa pay structure, and decided to gamble on Ormondroyd, Ian Olney, Tony Daley, Mountfield and, yes, Cowans.

Cowans and Bumstead stretch for a loose ball.

When Taylor left Cowans out of the side after only two matches, the player waited for four more and then responded. He was never a man for gestures, preferring to believe that in these circumstances a professional did the professional thing and played his way back into recognition. But Cowans was close to his 31st birthday and felt he had no time to waste in extended reserve team football, so he asked the manager what his prospects were. Had the answer been equivocal, there is little doubt that Cowans would have been on his way to his second English club, or maybe to Nantes who were interested at the time.

Possibly an act of self-assertion was vital to Cowans at this moment. The transformation in his play was amazing. Where previously he had behaved as if the vehicle behind him were short of wheels, now he could make his moves confident that there would not be disastrous goal-crashes. This, in turn, provided Platt with a source of intelligent passes and the knowledge that he could dart forward, sure that the central midfield was being closely guarded. The Cowans-Platt strategy, often with the intervention of Ormondroyd's head or Daley's speed, became feared throughout the League and although it was Platt who benefited with England caps, there isn't a Villa player who doesn't give half the credit to Cowans, who made the England 'B' side and just missed the World Cup flight again.

Platt himself said: 'Cowans is playing the best football of his life — and it is rubbing off on me. He's the real eye-opener. I haven't played alongside a better midfield exponent. His vision is unbelievable. I can go on a run and he spots it immediately. He must have eyes in the back of his head at times because his service is that accurate and on occasions uncanny. He hit a rough patch earlier this season but he just rolled up his sleeves and got on with the job of playing his way back.'

Cowans adds: 'The real difference this season is that we acquired one or two class players. That helped me enjoy myself more than ever. Maybe I don't score as much as I would like to but Platty is so good going into the box that I sit back 15-20 yards outside until he gets back. His runs are devastating, so nine times out of ten, he goes forward. As a team we became very difficult to beat this season. No-one could take us lightly.'

Cowans has earned everything he was ever given. Loyal, honest and modest, he was a born-again star last season, better at times than in his England days. In the home match with Forest, Platt marked Steve Hodge and Cowans was left to patrol the entire heartland of the pitch. He was the maestro that day, tireless and visionary. When I congratulated him, he said: 'I missed a few passes, I thought.'

A perfectionist, too.

Gordon Cowans

Born Durham 27th October 1958. Apprentice. Debut 7th February 1976. 1976-85 League appearances 277 (+ 10 subs) 42 goals. F.A. Cup 19 + 1/3. F.L. Cup 22 + 4/5. Europe 22 + 1/2. Total 340 + 16/52. 1988-90 League appearances 68 + 1, goals 8. F.A. Cup 10/0. F.L. Cup 6/0. Others 10/0. Total 94 + 1/8. Full totals: 345 + 11/50. F.A. Cup 29 + 1/3. F.L. Cup 28 + 4/5. Europe 22 + 1/2. Others 10. Total 434 + 17/60. 9 England caps (7 with Villa) 2 B Internationals, 5 under-21. F.L. Cup tankard 1977. League championship 1981, European Cup 1982, European Super Cup 1982. Young Player of Year 1980. Other club: Bari, Italy 1985-88. Sold £450,000, returned £250,000.

CHAPTER 11

David Platt

IF THE NEW AGE OF FOOTBALL IS ABOUT TOTAL players, about flexibility, athleticism, discipline, a good mind and rewards beyond the imaginations of men who were expected to be loyal on a car worker's wage, then David Platt is the archetypal modern man. He descends from the line founded by Johann Cryuff, although he would be the last to claim he possessed the Dutchman's capacity to orchestrate an entire game.

Nevertheless, Platt's liquid grace, his strength of purpose, his highly practical skills in midfield and his ability to score exceptional — often one-touch — goals made him one of the rages of the World Cup in Italy, England's secret weapons deployed just when the tournament thought our country's team had no more to offer.

A measure of his impact on the Italians was the telephone call I received the day after the final in Rome. It came from an Italian reporter anxious to unearth the most microscopic fact about this man who had sprung the trap on three defences of legendary parsimony. 'You see,' he said, 'while your papers are talking Gazza this and Gazza that, the one who impressed us was Platt. He can play and score goals. That makes him very valuable.'

How valuable? There followed the silence of shrugged shoulders. Then the reply: '£4, 4·5 million. Who knows? The Italian clubs will all be seeing what he can do next season.'

174

Platt's is one head which will remain unturned by talk of riches. His beginnings in professional football were so tenuous, the route so strewn with disappointments that he learned early that the glamour of football came in direct proportion to the hard work. An athlete with classic poise, his technique has been sharpened by Faldo-esque practice routines to the point where his single strike is comparable in penetration with that of the Open and US Masters champion.

There was nothing accidental about his positioning or the way he took those World Cup goals, the first, in the last minute of extra time against Belgium, of such import that with one kick he became a household name. Many people have cast doubt on the purity of that goal, suspecting it was a bit of a fluke. Yet those, such as Graham Taylor, would see it as no more than an extension of his Villa work, a young man rising to the occasion, following Paul Gascoigne's free-kick over his shoulder, turning and in one motion easing the volley wide of the goalkeeper. Had he swung wildly, mis-timed, caught the ball high on his right boot or tried to power it into goal, the result would have been negative. I can only think of Denis Law among British footballers who would have scored with such lethal grace.

His goal against the Cameroons in the quarter-final underlined his nose for a chance, as well as the remarkable way in which he had taken over from skipper Bryan Robson in the machine room of the side. Against the Africans, too, he discovered, I think, the essential difference between club and international football: that it takes more than sweat and toil to swamp the skills of men who race uninhibitedly with the ball. Platt did so much running in the first-half heat that the edge was lost from his pace soon after half-time.

By the third-place play-off in Bari, there was a new maturity to his game. His second consecutive headed goal was stunningly executed. Perfect in timing, direction and weight, it was another for the goal-of-the-tournament judges to ponder. By then, Platt, who had flown to Sardinia six weeks earlier admitting he was one of the worker ants, happy to be an alternative on the substitutes' bench, was a full-blown international footballer. And wallowing in it.

No reason why he shouldn't. As a modern, classless kind of man who, incidentally, is an astute watcher with an appreciation of what he should give and take from life, he has a real liking for people and their pecularities.

'David wants to learn,' said Taylor of him. 'He has an enormous number of qualities.' One of these, I might say, is to share the new England manager's sense of humour and recognition of the fact that football is not more important than life, even if it makes life worth living. Taylor, I suspect, was looking at Platt as a future England captain months before both became men of world renown, in July 1990.

How far he had travelled. Platt had gone from Oldham town boys' team to Manchester United YTS to Crewe Alexandra to Aston Villa and to England, always taunted by the idea that he was not good enough. Take his move to Villa: 'I was stuck in a hotel room for two weeks, wondering if I had taken on too much. Well, at Crewe I was top man and it was a buzz to be recognised in the street, that kind of thing. I had no right to expect to go straight into the first team who were, after all, top of the Second Division. I had been bought for £200,000 to strengthen the squad. That isn't a lot of money these days. Then I scored in my debut against Blackburn and although we lost I got another in the 5-2 win against Plymouth, and a third against Bournemouth made it three in three games.

'I was on my way. Then, with three matches to go, I had a tweak and missed Shrewsbury. Then Mark Lillis was injured so I was pushed into midfield and I scored an important goal when we beat Bradford. We secured promotion at Swindon — and what an afternoon that was — and I was also drafted into the under-21s tournament in Toulon. Things happened so quickly I hardly knew where I was. Then I had doubts about going into the First Division.'

He conceals his uncertainties with the skill of a salesman,

Platt poses with manager Graham Taylor on signing day.

for David Platt has the inner confidence of the man who has done his homework. When Kevin Keegan was at the summit of his powers, I remember a friend of mine claiming there were players with far more talent than Keegan, citing Rodney Marsh, Charlie George, Stan Bowles as men with natural ability of a higher order. I maintained that the greatest talent of all was to have refined what skills a man has to their sharpest point. Keegan did that, Bowles spent his time in the betting shop. Keegan was Borg to Nastase; Boycott to Jameson; fulfilment to promise.

Platt is a man who squeezes the talent out of himself. He learned he had to do that from an early age when his father, Frank, and elder brother, Anthony, used to coach him to swing his left foot on a playing field at Chadderton, Oldham. Anthony would roll the ball and David was allowed one touch before trying to beat his father with a left-foot shot.

What happened if he used his right? — 'I got a clip round the ear. Well, at least a good rollicking.'

Presumably, his father, now production director of *The Guardian* in London, saw more to the little fellow's potential than anyone else, for although David was left-winger in his school team, there were no selections for representative sides for half-a-dozen years.

When things happen to Platt they tend to happen at speed, a year or two of fallowness followed by a sudden dazzling fruitfulness. It was clear to supporters when in February, 1988, he first appeared for Villa that here was a player with an extra moment to do with the ball what he asked, to put in the early touch which is so vital in today's breakneck version of the game and to do so with natural balance, almost a parody of how coaches tell pupils they should do it.

Yet for all that, his first full season, when he was voted supporters' Player of the Year, rang boldly with promise. The devastating late runs which were to strike into the unprotected areas of so many defences a year later were no more than an occasional, tentative sally, more tabby than tiger. Bryan Robson was doing that kind of job, instinctively, when he was in his teens.

The truth is, of course, that Robson was a midfield player with attacking flair, Platt a forward who found he could defend. It is no accident that the two should be compared, for

Sheer concentration.

Platt's first club was Manchester United and his first League shirt the No. 7. He denies modelling himself on the England skipper, however, claiming that admiration was a long way short of idolatory. That is as maybe — and a player could hardly choose a better example — but Platt's game certainly has many elements of Robson's in it. He is not so outwardly aggressive and does not yet distribute so tellingly. Where they are similar is in those delayed bursts into the area, the non-stop commitment and their desire to take responsibility.

'Robson isn't fast but he has aggressive speed,' says Platt, whose own, greater pace has still to be allied to Robson's tactical and strategic skills. 'I was a lad with United where he was a first-team player but I never consciously modelled my game on his.'

Platt had been a United fan since his father took him along to Old Trafford as a boy. Frank's coaching gave his son a useful left foot. 'I am sure I would have been one-footed otherwise,' he says. 'My left foot will never be as good as Gordon Cowans's but I am grateful to my father. I don't recall too much about those early days except that I pestered my dad for boots and even jumped up and tried to hit him because I couldn't have any. He bought me some in the end, though.'

From Warneath Junior School, Oldham, he went to South Chadderton Comprehensive, eventually making the Oldham Schools team under-14s and 15s with whom he was regularly a substitute right-winger 'because they had found my left foot out.' Then in one of those characteristic spurts, things began to happen. He joined Chadderton and moved to centre-forward, progressing at such a rate that the youth who struggled for a team place was good enough a couple of years later to be encouraged by United to join them on the YTS scheme for training two nights a week. Three other Chadderton players went with him and after 12 months Platt was invited to become a YTS player, which was a place below apprentice in the pecking order. At that time United let Platt's Chadderton team-mate John Pemberton go. Pemberton went to Rochdale instead, later signing for Crystal Palace with whom he received a loser's medal in this year's F.A. Cup final.

Platt stayed a year and a half with United whose manager Ron Atkinson recognised the quality of a young professional

Brotherly love as Platt
and Derek Mountfield
celebrate a goal.

whose stylish touches and enthusiasm provoked a typical big-club dilemma. As a centre-forward Platt was sixth in a queue behind four internationals — Frank Stapleton, Norman Whiteside, Mark Hughes, Alan Brazil — and Nicky Wood, another young pro. Platt seldom made even the Central League side.

Crewe manager Dario Gradi, always probing the leftovers of the rich man's table, was invited by Atkinson to take Platt on loan. 'Good experience for him' was the general view and so the clean-cut young man took lodgings in Crewe and within a fortnight Gradi, who had originally promised Platt he would not offer him a contract during the loan period, broke his word and rang Atkinson with the offer to take Platt off his hands. Platt decided he preferred the Fourth Division to the

Lancashire League and was never to regret the move. No doubt
United do.

Atkinson had been wavering through the whole business.
Would he offer Platt another year-long contract in the
summer? Even he wasn't sure. So Platt went, taking
Atkinson's advice and a month's wage with him.

Platt says: 'I went back and the manager told me 'Just
keep working hard. I always liked you because you worked
hard. When you get a cap for England, remember what I told
you.' Then he gave me a month's wage, £350, in a packet. He
didn't have to do that. It was kind of him.'

Three years later, Atkinson remembered that conversa-
tion, too. He phoned me at my office to ask whether the Platt
sale to Villa was going through. 'I always had the feeling he
was going to make it,' he said. 'There was something about
him. I don't make too many mistakes but he was one.'

The intervening years at Gresty Road were Platt's
apprenticeship. Early on he scored a flush of goals and
attracted the attention of West Ham. Gradi told him he wasn't
ready for their level of football yet and promised to let him
know when he was, for Crewe deliberately polished young
players to sell as glittering jewels a few seasons later, whether
as cosmetic or the real thing was of no great importance to
managing director Gradi who was in the survival business.

By the summer of '87, Platt was shining brightly and
Gradi, who had taught the willing young learner so much about
football, had to persuade him to sign a year's contract for the
club to be able to cash in on a transfer fee. Platt did so, but
both had the feeling that by the next summer the player would
be elsewhere. Leicester were first to offer, their £60,000 soon
capped by Hull City with £100,000. Now the bidding was really
under way. Hibernian nodded next and when their £125,000
was refused they quickly topped it with another £25,000.
Meanwhile, Chelsea, Wolves, Watford and Aston Villa were
all waiting to pounce. First, though, Gradi took the Hibs bid to
his board and while he was doing this Graham Taylor took up
the running.

Platt leaps to make a connection.

Platt was sitting with team-mates when Gradi called him on to the pitch to tell him that a big club had come in for him. 'It's Aston Villa,' said the astute Londoner. The fee equalled Hibernian's but clearly Gradi was now trading up. Platt played for Crewe on the Saturday and against Sunderland in a Freight Rover match on Tuesday, expecting a call any moment. Finally, as Platt and Gradi discussed a further year's contract,

Taylor returned with a £200,000 bid. Checkmate. Although Platt asked for 48 hours to talk to his family and friends, there was never any serious doubt that he would land at Villa Park.

Taylor, for all the doubts he expressed about the size of the fee, was certain enough of his capture to settle a 3½-year contract with him. The Villa manager admitted, too, that had his assistant, Steve Harrison, not left to take over at Watford, he would not have been in such a hurry to sign the 22-year-old. Harrison, Taylor knew, also liked the potential.

In his own three years with Villa, Taylor signed up to three dozen men and in his full managerial career probably three or four times that number. Platt may yet prove to be his cleverest. The gold was pure, and not so completely fashioned that he and his coaches could not work him into new patterns. The fact that Platt urgently seeks perfection in himself makes the combination more rewarding, and perhaps in modern football a little unusual.

Recently Taylor said he liked big personalities off the field so long as they were big personalities on it as well. Big personalities without enough talent were a hole in the head.

When Platt joined Villa, he may well have revitalised Taylor's diminishing belief in the perfectibility of modern youth. Yes, there were exemplary young professionals at Bodymoor Heath — Tony Daley was a particular case — but few of those with the right attitude were good enough, and those with the wrong attitude were being moved on, faster than church jumble.

It is here, perhaps, that Taylor should be credited with the job he has done. Villa were not so much on the slide as over the precipice when Taylor joined them because, in the immortal phrase, 'they were there'. I am certain he left cosy Watford because he loved a scrap and that, if he could succeed in restoring a once-great heavyweight to the heights, then he would be ready for anything. Especially England. This is as honourable a motive as is to be found in football. What made it audacious was that Villa were in a fundamentally, if not financially, worse state than Crewe.

Returning to play against his former club, Crewe, Platt stretches to nudge his first goal.

Witnesses queue up with testimony. Andy Gray, Allan Evans and Nigel Spink agreed publicly that Villa were ripe to go right through the bottom, as they had 18 years earlier. Each had watched in despair as the drift from European Cup year, 1982, accelerated out of control under the management of Billy McNeill. Saunders's standards may sometimes have been tainted with injustice, but they were the proper standards of a football club and they worked. Subsequent managers had been dragged down by the weight of tradition and dissension in the club. Players perceived that the power base had shifted from the manager's brick-walled little office at Bodymoor to the carpeted capaciousness of the North Stand first floor at Villa Park.

To his credit, Doug Ellis either realised this or, at least, sensed that what his friends had been telling him might have been true — Villa needed a manager with the authority to manage. When, completely out of the blue, Graham Taylor telephoned to let him know he was available, the salmon-fishing chairman hooked the biggest catch of his life. He hung on to him, too. To my undying embarrassment, I was tipped off that Taylor was prime candidate for the job a week before the actual announcement but found it so hard to pin down that my newspaper used only one paragraph suggesting that he might, just, be in the running. Dave Bassett was the name everyone followed, right up to a couple of hours before the press conference revelation.

If that joke was on the press, most of the others were on Taylor. Villa's youth development programme appeared to have malfunctioned — this was not altogether so because several players, such as Ian Olney and Mark Blake, were coming through — and for all that the older playing staff looked adequate for the Second Division, careful study revealed players of declining ability and some of weak character, too. Of the 26 players used to gain promotion in his first season, only four of the current staff played under McNeill. Taylor made ten first-team signings, of whom only three are still with the club. This wasn't so much a turnover as a whole new pie, for of the entire backroom staff only boot man Jim Paul remains.

Platt became part of the revolution in February. He made friends with the crowd quickly and until March 26, Villa were cruising towards the championship. Then, suddenly, with the 1-0 home defeat by Stoke, they froze. Experienced men were finding the tension too great, and one point out of 12, this from a goal scored by Platt at Crystal Palace, had them buckling three matches from the end. Two twitchily nervous home victories followed against Shrewsbury and Bradford, against whom Platt headed a fine goal. Leaving behind scenes of premature celebration, we all drove to Swindon on May 7, half hoping for automatic promotion but expecting to have to depend on the torn safety-net of the play-offs.

That game at the County Ground was among the most remarkable I have witnessed, not because it was good — in fact it was drab — but because it reaffirmed the absolute unpredictability of the game. Villa, we felt, had to win, otherwise either Middlesbrough or Bradford would overtake them, provided Middlesbrough drew or Bradford won. Middlesbrough were leading at half-time and then, when the whistle blew on a 0-0 draw at Swindon, were a goal down to Leicester City. The word went out from the 5,000 Villa fans crushed into one tiny corner of the ground that Middlesbrough had succumbed, so had Bradford despite a late rally to 2-3 against Ipswich, and, therefore, Villa were promoted.

It wasn't true at all. The Ayresome Park game had been delayed by seven minutes and, as this fact dawned on Taylor, his players and their supporters, a hush spread like wind across wheat. There were further false alarms, too, before finally a radio in the dressing room reported that Villa had been promoted, not on points, not on goal difference but on the 68 goals scored compared with Middlesbrough's 63.

Platt remembers: 'You would hardly have bet on a sequence of results like those. The crowd went wild at our finish and the stewards ran on to say we were up. We were celebrating while they were still playing . . . unbelievable. Then we were up and the proper celebrations started. I recall thinking that if Steve Harrison hadn't left Villa, the gaffer wouldn't have been in a hurry to sign me and I wouldn't have been sitting there with a cup of champagne in my hand, toasting us and promotion. Then I began to have the usual doubts about stepping up.

'When I look back now I realise how the gaffer had to keep us happy after the defeats by Stoke, Millwall and Oldham. I suppose the pressure got to us but I never actually thought that. These things must be subconscious because you only have to think what happened to Leeds last season to know something is at work. They were coasting it and then only managed to go up in the last game of the season.'

As the bubbles in the champagne subsided, Taylor settled down in a corner of the County Ground away team dressing room and against the background of excited horseplay made the serious point that he would require £2 million to spend for Villa to have a chance of finishing in the top six of the First Division the following season. Little did he know Villa were to survive by a solitary point and that the end of 1988-89 season would be even more fraught than the one passing, a mirror image of tension as applied at the bottom of the table compared with the top.

During the summer, Taylor spent about a third of the sum he had proposed, and although the purchases of Derek Mountfield from Everton, Gordon Cowans from Bari, and Chris Price, from Blackburn, were successful in the longer term, they did no more than help secure a passable first half of the season. The revelation of this period was Alan McInally, an imposing Scot with a trundling style that, given room, would develop into an unstoppable juggernaut. One of his goals, in a League Cup defeat of Millwall, won goal-of-the-season awards and would be candidate in most people's best top ten of all time. McInally transformed the inside-right channel into a goal trail, striking twenty by the time Santa Claus had snow on his boots.

Alongside him, Platt was learning about the First Division. Platt was occasionally moved into midfield but generally his was a support role between McInally and any of three or four wingers. He scored four goals against Ipswich in a Littlewoods Cup match. These helped take the team into the last eight of the competition, so that by January, aided by an extraordinary and, for Platt a nostalgic, 3-2 victory at Crewe, Taylor had a right to feel satisfied with the results so far. Then, inside ten days, Villa were knocked out of the Littlewoods Cup at West Ham, out of the F.A. Cup by Wimbledon, and left with nothing to strive for but respectability and the shoreline nearly four months away. They only just made it. Taylor's luck held.

P.F.A. Footballer
of the Year.

Platt says: 'We were confident before these defeats and then confidence went out of the side.' McInally's goal streak ran out and the introduction of two wingers, Nigel Callaghan and Ian Ormondroyd, for £1,150,000, confused their new colleagues far more than the opposition. Taylor had decided his team needed fresh impetus and, instead, they ground to a halt. Neither held his place to the end of the season and the frustration of the crowd at the increasingly desperate efforts of both soon transferred itself to their team-mates. Through all the turmoil, Platt alone enhanced his reputation and although it was last season that he made large, black capital letters in the newspapers, for me he became a footballer of standing when the storm broke in the previous March, April and May.

He was to be seen undemonstratively urging further effort

from his colleagues and I am afraid Callaghan lost his last trace of respect from the home crowd when Platt was once seen to be signalling to the winger that he should have chased a pass to the by-line. Callaghan's deceptively casual style is not what Villa fans were brought up on.

Villa finished the season wretchedly, leaving themselves one ahead of Middlesbrough on 40 points when the last referee blew the final whistle. Few fans saw West Ham as a danger to their team's interests, for the East Londoners required nine points from the remaining three matches they still had. The Hammers promptly won two of those, including a superb victory at Forest, and when Platt drove from Heathrow after the Monday night return of the England B tourists, a win by West Ham at Anfield would have relegated his side.

He says: 'You had to fancy Liverpool to win, especially as they were chasing the championship. I dropped off Dave Sexton in Coventry and turned on the radio to hear that Liverpool were a goal ahead. All of a sudden, I was happy, then Rosenoir equalised and for ten minutes West Ham swarmed all over them. Wardy hit the bar and I couldn't listen any more. Eventually, I flicked it on again and Liverpool were 2-1 ahead, then it was 3-1 and I knew I could relax. There was no way West Ham were going to score three goals. In the end, Liverpool won 5-1 but I was left with mixed emotions. It was tremendous that we stayed up, but we needed our bums kicking for ever being in that position, sweating on West Ham's last fixture. Then it was next season and a new start.'

The summer buy-and-sell spree on which Taylor embarked was critical and daring in that Villa lost two players, McInally and Martin Keown, regarded by most supporters as vital elements in the team. Taylor thought otherwise, and although he made an effort to keep Keown, he had no qualms about letting McInally go to Bayern Munich, just as he had willingly sold the highly talented Andy Gray to QPR. Taylor puts team before individual; dependability above flamboyance. And anyway, he had made his own £2 million this time.

Upon one point those old adversaries Ellis and Saunders had always agreed — equal pay for senior players. They may have done so for different reasons, I suspect, but for a dozen years equal pay plus bonuses were the rule, even if this was a facade in that there were differentials in signing-on fees and loyalty bonuses out of all proportion to the loyalty shown. Taylor didn't accept this reasoning and that summer, Ellis and Taylor had a showdown. Had Taylor threatened to walk out, that would have been no surprise, either. Whether this was his bluff, or he changed the chairman's mind by other persuasion we may never know, but by August, Ellis had acquiesced. There would no longer be a basic-wage policy at Villa Park.

This, Taylor avers, is the Big Club stance. Fewer stars means larger wages — that is the irrevocable law of supply and demand, the fulcrum of capitalism, and nothing in this life is more capitalistic than a major football club. Managers thrive on it, or manage nothing. Taylor went straight out and bought Paul McGrath and Kent Nielsen. By the end of the next season, Platt had three years more on his contract, Tony Daley five, while others, too, enjoyed even better relationships with their bank managers.

The McGrath and Nielsen transfers were at the heart of Villa's achievement last season, for the three-man central defence — Mountfield made up the third — turned out to be the opposition's flexible enemy. 'The gaffer says he came across the system by accident,' says Platt, 'but he had to be clever enough to think of it and brave enough to try it.'

Taylor also chose to settle Platt in central midfield with Cowans, and made one final attempt to extract the best from Daley, even if it meant abandoning Callagan and, late in the season, Ormondroyd. Thus are creativeness and confession — for surely this was Taylor's admission of error — good for the soul. Platt scored 24 goals, all but a handful as a midfielder, and formed a partnership with Cowans that dazzled the First Division.

'Gordon is the best footballer I have ever played alongside,' says Platt.

'David is a natural footballer. He can run forever. He's very fit and quick, good in the air, has a strong tackle and can hold players off with his strength,' says Cowans, who with assistant manager John Ward, often stays late to help sharpen Platt's finishing. Shades of Frank and Anthony 14 years earlier in Chadderton.

Only a year or so ago Platt refused to commit himself as to his favourite position. Today he says: 'Midfield is my best spot and I would like to settle there for a while. Mind you, I don't half enjoy myself up front when I score a few goals. Sometimes the midfield's a slog and the gaffer is bound to shove me up front.

'I look at versatility as an advantage because if I'm having a bad game at least he can shift my position. I've been given a free role in the centre by Villa, although obviously we all have to be disciplined as a team. I know people said I man-for-man marked sometimes last season, particularly when we played Forest. That wasn't true. Steve Hodge and I were doing the same kind of job and we both have to battle. I can't stop running and he can't stop me running but when he went deep I had to go deep with him or he'd score goals.'

Three draws, a win and three defeats, culminating in a thrilling Trevor Francis hat-trick for QPR at Villa, appeared to be an early-season warning that Villa were going to hang around the lower half of the table for the whole course. Platt had opened with six goals in eight games yet, oddly, failed in the next four just when the tempo of their season was lifted. Then the TV cameras dwelt on them for 90 minutes of the match with Everton at Villa Park on November 5 and the memory of explosive action lit up the whole season for Villa fans. Everton lost 6-2, Platt and Ian Olney each scored twice, and Platt still looks annoyed at the idea of giving away the couple to Everton late on.

He says: 'We were getting a local reputation but nationally we weren't regarded as anything special until that game. I should have had a hat-trick. I'm certain it was the performance

Platt beats Shilton for a classic goal.

that got me into the England squad for the Italy game. We lost
to West Ham in the Littlewoods Cup and to Norwich in the
League straight afterwards. Our confidence was still high,
though, and we won three before coming across Liverpool. We
drew and it was there, I think, we began to believe we could
take the League title. At half-time we were 1-0 up and I fancied
us to get another. We made a mistake then of lying back and

inviting them to have a go. They really got at us from every angle and we were fortunate in the end to come away with a point. Peter Beardsley reckoned we deserved a draw, though, for our first half.

'Obviously Liverpool have the best players in the country, yet the season was much closer than it looks if you just check the League table. Anyone going to the club knows that not only will they get the best terms but they can offer a trophy or two every season as well. Liverpool and me? I have no thoughts about it. I want to stay here and help win things for Villa. I know that in my, say, eight years with Villa we can't be on a par with them because they have been at the top for 20 years but we can make a very good start on it.'

By the New Year, Platt had scored 17 goals, made his international debut and Villa had headed the First Division. On December 30, with one instant twist, controlling the ball inside the area, he threw three Arsenal defenders into knee-jolting imbalance before beating goalkeeper John Lukic with a crisp little shot to remind us that not only Van Basten has the gift of a ballet master's poise. Italia 90 was to view the same lethal finishing skill seven months later.

The Villa charge lasted to February 21. Platt had been given the pleasure of a goal against Manchester United in a splendid 3-0 Boxing Day win at Villa Park, while Chelsea were dispatched by the same score at Stamford Bridge on New Year's Day. Zenith Cup defeats by Middlesbrough, due to escape relegation from the Second Division by a slim margin, caused a minor stir, yet when Villa went to White Hart Lane to record their seventh consecutive League victory by goals from Ormondroyd and Platt, the five-point advantage held over Liverpool seemed about to become decisive.

Wimbledon! Oh, what deeds are done in thy name! On February 24, they visited Birmingham and stunned a 29,000 crowd by simply outplaying the League leaders. Had Platt not missed an early penalty, driving the ball against the goalkeeper's legs, maybe these final paragraphs would read differently. Maybe. But I doubt it. The outstanding professionalism at White Hart Lane had given way to a distracted, almost numb Villa, short of aggression and passion. They offered nothing.

'The Bubble Has Burst' exclaimed newspapers throughout the country and, although there were moments when it seemed they might still deny Liverpool, I am afraid those headlines told the truth, except that it wasn't a dramatic burst but a gradual exhalation. Seven goals in 11 games and heavy defeat by Oldham in an F.A. Cup quarter-final were only aggravated by the fact that £1.5 million striker Tony Cascarino was not immediately successful in correcting the grievous fault of failure to take chances. Further defeats by Crystal Palace, Manchester City, where Villa had their worry beads out for a live TV audience to see, and Manchester United, were too much to contend with, and so the second-to-last Saturday of the season brought Norwich to Villa Park where Villa had to win. A goal down at half-time, for 20 minutes afterwards the brilliance that had enthralled millions on November 5 was on show again. Cascarino scored his first goal for Villa, Daley and Platt added others. At least, it seemed, Villa would have the consolation of taking Liverpool into the last week. Norwich scored twice, instead, and the last speck of hope was blown away.

If Villa's symphony ended too soon, the same was not true of Platt's. Once in the England squad, he was not to be budged, for clearly Bobby Robson's verdict was much the same as Cowans's and his own: that there is a good deal more to come from a player who never stops trying to learn. 'I suppose my particular attribute is that I was always prepared to give up anything to be a better footballer,' he says. 'My greatest honour before the World Cup was to play for my country against Brazil whom everyone in football regards as THE team no matter who won in Italy. And to go to the World Cup seemed unbelievable when you think that three years ago I was a Fourth Division player.

'As I say, 90 minutes against Brazil is every lad's dream. I think I had a reasonable game without setting the world alight in that No 7 shirt. I'd like to think I have a lot of defensive qualities as well as being able to score. Playing Brazil demands discipline but I think if a team play confidently they can get on top and worry them into allowing gaps and holes.'

His words were prophetic. But by the end of the World Cup, even that Brazil experience had become just another step towards great deeds. Rarely can a player have made such an entrance to the international stage and, remember, he had also in late winter been named the PFA Footballer of the Year. His goals in Italy — the first by a Villa player in the World Cup — also proclaimed that the old Villa Lions were back on their feet again and that Europe had nothing to fear but their football.

Like Bryan Robson and Peter Shilton, Platt is a racehorse owner. His good looks split into a smile as wide as Joe E. Brown's when he talks of General Silky, the five-year-old jumper he describes as 'a big baby'. The General hasn't provided David, girlfriend Rachel and their small syndicate with a victory yet. But he is confident and he has all the ability to be a winner. So, unquestionably, has David Platt.

David Platt

Born 7th July 1966. Signed from Crewe Alexandra for £200,000. Debut 20th February 1988. League appearances 85, goals 30. F.A. Cup 7/2. FL Cup 9/7. Others 7/4. Total 108/43. 10 England caps. International goals 3. World Cup finals squad 1990. Midlands Player of the Year (jointly with Paul McGrath) 1989-90. Other clubs: Manchester United, Crewe.

Aston Villa Facts

Aston Villa's record since the war is:

League campions: 1980-81; runners-up: 1989-90.

Division Two champions: 1959-60.

Division Three champions: 1971-72.

League sequences: Division One (from 1946-47 to 1958-59): 12, 8, 6, 10, 12, 15, 16, 11, 13, 6, 20, 10, 14, 21 (relegated). Division Two (1959-60): 1. Division One (1960-61 to 1966-67): 9, 7, 15, 19, 16, 16, 21 (relegated). Division Two (1967-68 to 1969-70): 16, 18, 21 (relegated). Division Three (1970-71 to 1971-72): 4, 1. Division Two (1972-73 to 1974-75): 3, 14, 2. Division One (1975-76 to 1986-87): 16, 4, 8, 8, 7, 1, 11, 6, 10, 10, 16, 22 (relegated). Division Two (1987-88): 2. Division One (1988-89 to 1989-90): 17, 2.

F.A. Cup winners: 1956-57.

League Cup winners: 1960-61, 1974-75, 1976-77.

European Cup winners: 1981-82.

Record home gate: 76,588 v Derby County (F.A. Cup).